# HAMLET'S TWIN

# HAMLET'S TWIN
## by Hubert Aquin

translated by Sheila Fischman

McCLELLAND AND STEWART

This translation is for H. R. with love and gratitude

Originally published as *Neige Noire*,
copyright © 1974 by Hubert Aquin.
This translation by Sheila Fischman, *Hamlet's Twin*,
copyright © 1979 by McClelland and Stewart Limited

*The Canadian Publishers*
McClelland and Stewart Limited
25 Hollinger Road
Toronto M4B 3G2

CANADIAN CATALOGUING IN PUBLICATION DATA

Aquin, Hubert, 1929-1977.
  [Neige noire. English]
  Hamlet's twin

Translation of Neige noire.

ISBN 0-7710-0800-7

I. Title.   II. Title: Neige noire.   English.

PS8501.Q56N413   C843'.5'4   C79-094002-7
PQ3919.2.A66N413

This translation was completed with the support of
The Canada Council

Printed and bound in Canada
by John Deyell Company

The city is sweltering, as it has been all summer. Montreal is like a vast open furnace: apartment windows are wide open, offering solitary voyeurs countless low-angle views. Bare shoulders, backs exposed to the sun, thighs spread open, faces coated with sun-tan lotion, white stomachs: so many components of dizzying allusive images! An acid taste of sun-reddened epidermis suffuses the fleeting image. All the strangers at the windows are blinded by the light, while down below the others, clothes sticking to their skin, hug the walls in search of shade, many thinking only of the moment when they will be able to take off every bit of clothing, no matter how light. The sultry heat has created a sort of fascination few people can escape, which reduces the movement of life to a listless stasis.

When night comes Sylvie and Nicolas are lying on their backs in bed, naked, dripping wet, broken. Sylvie gives in to sleep; her eyes grow heavy, her breathing becomes deeper and more regular. Her right hand is at the top of her thigh, at the most vulnerable place on her body, as though to veil the invisible. Nicolas gets up quietly, glancing at Sylvie to be sure she really is asleep. In sleep she is very beautiful. A small rivulet of sweat flows between her breasts and forms a pearly river around her neck.

Nicolas locks himself in the bathroom and takes a cold shower. The cold water affords him a certain relief and he examines himself thoroughly as it flows over him. The bluish spot is there, swollen by the erection that still possesses him. Whenever he has an erection he experiences a shooting pain on the left side of his penis, at the frenum, and whenever the hyperesthesic tension of the penis lets up there is a pinching sensation.

Nicolas' suffering is sapping his strength. Circles under his eyes, fatigue, lack of muscle tone, relentless despondency: all this can be seen, so description is superfluous. And the image reflected on the screen reveals, in the end, only as much as the words of a hermetic poem.

Insert still photographs of Pyramiden in the scene in the shower. When Nicolas looks closely at himself in the mirror, use the same process and insert still shots of the Chain of the Seven Glaciers. Finally, alternate closeups of Nicolas (circles under the eyes, moles, freckles) with still shots of the crevasses on Cape Mitra.

Nicolas returns to the bedroom, cool now. He sits in an armchair across the room from Sylvie who is still asleep. Flashback: closeup of Nicolas: we see him lifting his head over Sylvie's shoulder, then withdrawing from her, grimacing with pain. Both are naked, of course. Shoot this scene in daylight so that the photographs and prints on the walls of Nicolas' apartment can be seen. The viewer understands that for some time now sexual relations have been very frustrating for Nicolas; not just frustrating, impossible!

His life has been reduced to an intolerable series of discomforts. Really, it would be better for him not to look at Sylvie, who is wearing no garment but her sleep. For the slightest excitement is disastrous and Nicolas' long deprivation has only increased his over-stimulation and suffering. In the time it takes to sketch out this explanation, Nicolas feels the premonitory symptoms of an erection and a few seconds later the shooting pain he dreads so much. This time he nearly faints and crumples to the floor, dazed, his cheek against the minium-coloured nap of the rug. The camera also turns away. Blackout.

July 16, 1973. Nicolas leaving the apartment around 3:00 p.m. From the balcony Sylvie can see Nicolas on the sidewalk. She watches him walk down towards Sherbrooke Street.

Cut to rehearsal studio 5, level B, Maison de Radio-Canada. A ninety-minute television drama is being rehearsed: Shakespeare's *Hamlet*. But Nicolas is not playing the title role, which has been given, as is only fitting, to Jean-Louis Roux. When Shakespeare wrote *Hamlet* he was thinking of someone rather like Jean-Louis Roux, not Burbage. Nicolas sits down with one of his fellow actors.

NICOLAS
What will happen to Hamlet when Jean-Louis Roux is old enough to play the ghost?

ACTOR
Come on, you know Jean-Louis Roux would never agree to play a dead man...

They laugh. Nicolas is playing Fortinbras.


(Fortinbras...Just what does he signify at this point? And who among the spectators knows that Fortinbras is the Prince of Norway and son of Fortinbras, ruler of Norway and former enemy of Hamlet's father? It's difficult, of course, to translate these dynastic rivalries into shots, but nothing's impossible. So keep these notes on Fortinbras, don't forget that Fortinbras is probably an enemy of Claudius and a potential ally of Claudius' murderer. In the end, Fortinbras finally succeeds where Laertes and Hamlet fail. He avenges his father by winning back the kingdom of Denmark in his name. Three vengeful sons, only one victorious: Fortinbras.)

Nicolas, like all the other actors, attends the dress rehearsals that precede the taping, expected to take place on July 19 and 20 at CIR-1. Jean-Louis Roux, Linda Noble, Francis Augé, Albert Millaire, and Georges Groulx are already in the rehearsal studio when Stanislas Parisé, the producer, arrives. The ritual of greetings proceeds with the usual obsequiousness. Nicolas, in his corner, is reading his lines: about 30 in all, 40 at the most.

FORTINBRAS

Where is this sight?

HORATIO    (Nicolas reads the cue)
What is it you would see?
If aught of woe or wonder, cease your search.

FORTINBRAS

This quarry cries on havoc...

Fortinbras' part is a thin one, the character rich. But Nicolas acts no better when he has fewer words to say; in fact, his acting is worse. Speeches that are so rare and so important upset him. He is unable to muster his aplomb in so few words.

FORTINBRAS

I have some rights of memory in this kingdom,
Which now to claim my vantage doth invite me.

STAN PARISÉ

Don't tell me that's the way you talk when you order a beer in a tavern!

NICOLAS

Terribly sorry, Stan, but Fortinbras isn't ordering a beer in that line. He's declaring his rights over the kingdom of Denmark and announcing that he intends to exercise those rights.

STANISLAS

What's this? Are you trying to give us a lecture on Elizabethan theatre or naturalism? Start again.

He stands in front of Nicolas and waits. After a long silence Nicolas begins again in a low, monotonous voice.

NICOLAS

I have some rights of memory in this kingdom,
Which now to claim my vantage doth invite me....There, I said it as naturally as somebody ordering a beer. And you still aren't happy, Stan. You know what I think? You have to emphasize the declamatory tone in Fortinbras' lines, not try to make him talk like everybody else. Fortinbras should be pompous, otherwise he doesn't stand out.

Imperturbable, Stan Parisé sits on a folding chair a few feet from Nicolas.

STAN

Page 147, Fortinbras' first line. Let's go.

NICOLAS

Where is this sight?

STAN

Again.

NICOLAS

Where is this sight?

STAN

Once more.

NICOLAS

What's got into you?

STAN

Again.

NICOLAS

Where is this sight?

(The silence is uncomfortable, disagreeable. End this sequence without ending it: emphasize its weighty character, give it an overdose of silence. The spectator doesn't know the characters in the film yet, at least not in any way except by the physical existence of the actors. It is a mediatized knowledge. The important thing at this stage is not to give a physical description of each character but rather to have a general intuitive feeling about him. Later, during the script development, the cast will have to be established; doing so too soon would predetermine the course of the plot and interfere with its inception.)

Nicolas leaves studio 5 around midnight. Dissolve to rue Sainte-Catherine at the corner of Saint-Denis or Papineau. Drug peddlers and queers cross paths on the sidewalk. No women, or very few, and they are all with men. Nicolas walks past a series of establishments more or less connected with one another: nightclubs, discothèques, restaurants, topless bars, *brasseries*. Parallel travelling shot: a stream of cars and taxis; then, on the other side of the street, the same kind of establishments all crowded together.

Flashes of fog at the approach to Båtvika.

Nicolas looks in the window of a topless bar. We can distinguish blueish landscapes, nude dancers, haunches swaying, thrashing about in clouds of smoke; furtive glances, turned backs, people smoking, bodies touching.

Intermittent flashes: the Beerenberg emerging from the mists, sinister, solemn, motionless.

Four more days, Nicolas thinks, and it will be finished, recorded, taped, in the can. Five days and I take it from the top. Then there'll be nothing but trees, roofs, glaucous beds, formless winding paths, rectilinear cadastral surveys, bits of road, miniaturized houses! Just five more days and a few hours and there will be a broken ice floe, its fractures infinitesimal, then the scattered masses of Svalbard, land at last and, just before we arrive, the bronze waters of the Bunde.

Sylvie is sleeping peacefully. She is naked, her closed fists between her thighs. Nicolas puts his script on the dresser, goes into the kitchen. He mixes himself a gin and orange juice and sits on the living-room sofa. The television is spitting out something he's already seen; Nicolas takes a quick inventory of the programs available by turning the dial. He leaves it on Channel 3.

Fade to bathroom. The camera is on a dolly at a right angle to the basin and at the same level. Nicolas enters, turns on the light, takes his penis out of his undershorts. There is still a swelling on the left side, near the glans. Very cautiously he places his penis on the edge of the basin and spreads some cold-cream on the sore. Afterwards he looks in the mirror and makes all sorts of faces: he strikes poses, puts on airs, all the time observing himself. A real actor!

NICOLAS
Where is this sight? Where is this sight? Where is this sight?

He continues his voice exercises. The camera shoots him from another angle, as though it were over his shoulder.

Alternating superimpositions of the crevasses of Cape Mitra. Give an uninterrupted lateral movement to the inserted shots of Cape Mitra and a formal paralysis to the framing of the bathroom. Another change of shots: those of Nicolas are frozen while his reflection in the mirror is kinetic. The only synchronism between him and his reflection occurs when he says: "Where is this sight?" As soon as he has said it, the two images are separated, establishing a psychological loss of focus which is not corrected by the flashes of Cape Mitra.

Sylvie appears in the doorway. Nicolas sees her in the mirror, then turns around to kiss her. Sylvie has put on her pyjama top.

SYLVIE

It's late, isn't it...

NICOLAS

Around twelve-thirty.

SYLVIE

And how's Hamlet coming along?

NICOLAS

We'll soon be finished.

He turns out the bathroom light, puts his arm around Sylvie to lead her back to bed. She takes off her pyjama top and lies down on the sheets. Nicolas has never seen her look so beautiful. Her blonde hair spread over the pillow like an octopus, her skin amber, her arms thrown back and breasts upthrust.

SYLVIE

What is it, Nic? Aren't you coming to bed?

NICOLAS

Later! I'm not sleepy yet.

Rapid, flashing shots: Sylvie's breasts, her open mouth, her hair tangled in Nicolas' fingers, her armpits, belly, legs. Nicolas' look of suffering. He can distinguish only Sylvie's ghostly silhouette on the bed (which he is walking away from) – a firm-breasted odalisque with tapering legs. Her beauty provokes a flood in his spongy depths. Nicolas turns his head, puts his hand on his pe-

nis as though he has been hit in the groin. He is motionless for a moment, contorted with pain.

SYLVIE

Let's put off our trip, Nicolas. I don't want to see you in that
state when we're travelling.

NICOLAS

It's getting better, Sylvie. Everything will be over by the
twentieth, I know it will. No, we have to leave when we
planned; it will be a kind of break between before and after.

SYLVIE

What do you mean?

NICOLAS

Our life is going to change, love. Even professionally, everything's going to change. Before, I was an actor; after our trip, I
won't be. When you're twenty-eight there's still time to
change careers and that's what I'm going to do. But everything I've done so far won't be wasted because I'm going to
work in films. Fortinbras is my last role.

(The viewer has the feeling that the film he is watching is
being turned inside out and that Fortinbras will soon cease to
exist. The actors were characters, but now one of the characters is deciding to stop being an actor.)

NICOLAS

We're leaving in a few days. And as soon as I'm back I'm
going into production of my first film with Marcus Films.

SYLVIE

I'm afraid...

NICOLAS

What?

SYLVIE

Yes, I'm afraid when everything starts to change; our life's been changing for some time now, the two of us have changed a lot...And now all of a sudden, a few days before we leave, I find out that you're changing careers...I'm afraid. It isn't rational, I know.

(Stretch out this dialogue a little. Be sure to accentuate the fuzziness of the words exchanged by Sylvie and Nicolas. Keep Sylvie in closeup during the dialogue. At no time does Nicolas come close to her – and this too contributes to the possibly agonizing effect of the scene.)

Nicolas in the living-room in front of the television set which is still on, but silent. The screen gives off only a formless magma, striated, in a herring-bone pattern, with irregular chrominance. What is represented on the screen represents nothing at all.

NICOLAS

Another four days and I'll be flying over moving, undecipherable images.

End the sequence on Nicolas asleep in front of the television set from which a multicoloured lava is flowing. Fade to a still shot of Nathorst.

Cut. Rehearsal studio 5, level B. Linda Noble, who is playing Ophelia, is young, svelte, elegant: a true reincarnation of Katherine Hamlett! Nicolas, gazing hypocritically at her, finds she bears a certain resemblance to Sylvie.

(And as there can be only optical solutions in films, a shot of Sylvie must be superimposed on the one of Linda Noble. The

14

two images are not in focus at the same time, as though vainly seeking each other.)

Medium shot of Linda Noble as Polonius reads to Gertrude Hamlet's poem to Ophelia.

POLONIUS

Doubt that the stars are fire;
   Doubt that the sun doth move;
Doubt truth to be a liar;
   But never doubt I love.

Linda Noble rehearses her movements with Polonius; silent sequence. The choreography is slower than slow. As accompaniment, Nicolas' voice this time.

NICOLAS

Doute que l'étoile soit flamme
Doute du soleil et du jour
Doute si vérité trahit l'âme
Ne doute pas de mon amour.

Alternate shots of Linda rehearsing her movements and of Sylvie turning over in bed. Over these shots, which follow one another, begin again and finally overlap, with Linda's voice now repeating Hamlet's poem.

LINDA

Doute que les étoiles soient de feu
Doute que le soleil se meuve
Doute de la vérité même
Ne doute pas que je t'aime.

The camera stays on Linda Noble, sitting near Nicolas: they watch the other actors working under Stan Parisé's direction.

POLONIUS

That he is mad, 'tis true: 'tis true 'tis pity
And pity 'tis 'tis true –

15

STAN PARISÉ

That Polonius is brilliant, 'tis true...But when that speech gets off to such a rotten start I need a ten-minute break to get my head together. Idem, everybody, take ten.

Stan Parisé gives the actors a blasé look.

STAN PARISÉ

Ten minutes, OK?

Stan Parisé is facing Nicolas, who is looking in another direction: Stan follows his look, which leads to Linda Noble. The frame tightens on Linda Noble. Stan goes over to Nicolas.

STAN PARISÉ

How come you haven't had her? Everybody else has.

NICOLAS

What are you going to come up with next?

Nicolas leaves the rehearsal studio and goes to an underground lobby in the Radio-Canada building. He goes into a telephone booth and dials a number. Cut.

A large bedroom. The breeze blowing in through the French windows lifts the muslin curtains.

Cut back to the telephone booth: Nicolas is waiting, waiting, waiting. He hangs up, collects his dime and starts again. Shots of another bedroom: the telephone rings once, twice, three times. Swish pan to the bed, which has not even been slept in.

Flashes: Nicolas dialing again.

The large bedroom: we can make out Sylvie's naked arm embracing an unidentified partner.

(Each imagined sequence with Sylvie must be longer than the preceding one; in this way the viewer will be increasingly overcome by what is disturbing Nicolas. On the other

16

hand, the inset sequences in the telephone booth should be increasingly short, rather as though Nicolas Vanesse is being shipwrecked in hydrocyanic bird-lime.)

Closeup of Nicolas holding the telephone: he closes his eyes as he hangs up.

The large bedroom. We can make out the shape of the bed, a single naked entwined form. Freeze shot: use blue filter. ECU of Nicolas' right ear, then swish pan to his left eye. Flashes of the Hornsundtind.

The large bedroom. Zoom in on the bed. Slow motion (72 frames/second) of Sylvie shaken by a series of spasms while her partner, seen from the back, enters her steadily, kissing her mouth, breasts and neck. Sylvie emits a moan, which must be transformed into diffracted waves. The image switches to negative when the wave reaches its peak.

In the telephone booth: Nicolas seems to hear Sylvie's moans through the receiver.

The large bedroom. A series of waves runs through Sylvie's body. Nicolas leaves the telephone booth. Closeup of him walking through the lobby among the other actors.

The large bedroom. The shots of Sylvie and her partner take on a hallucinating quality, almost saturnalian. Sylvie, open-mouthed, completely abandoned, moves frenetically until the man has his orgasm. She seems to be having a second orgasm as she holds him with her hands flat on his lower back. Nicolas' voice reverberates over these images in an echo-chamber.

NICOLAS

Woe is me for having seen, for seeing, what I have seen, what I see!

(From this moment the film must attain a new level: that of compression.)

> Rehearsal studio. Zoom in on Linda Noble who is saying her lines. The shots of Linda are multiplied by a multitude of angles and at an ever-increasing rate. Nicolas watches her closely and insistently.

(Linda is a screen-character: she reflects. But nothing passes through her, particularly not light. Nicolas keeps looking at her, but all he can do is enumerate the garments she is wearing, their colours which range from cinnabar to a deathly blue, delineate her eyes, follow the line of her legs. He is restricted to her surface, her mask. The film coincides very closely with this cortical perception of reality. Besides, this cinematographic specificity is infinitely seductive: it resembles each person's aleatory adventure. Life does not make it possible to go very far, nor to go deeply into the meaning of all that exists. The human being, no matter how gifted he is, always remains outside whatever he wishes to break through, just like Nicolas, who thinks he is stripping Linda of her clothes merely by running his eyes over her – a step which need not be made explicit, since it corresponds so satisfactorily to every filmic structure. When Nicolas has taken this inventory of Linda, nothing has really filtered through. And the unforeseeable may come about. After all, the movie is only a historiated strip of film; there is absolutely no need for it.)

> Stanislas Parisé's apartment. It is around 2:00 p.m. The scene takes place in the guest room. Linda is partially bound to the metal posts of the bed on which she is lying completely naked. Nicolas holds the rope, tying it firmly.

LINDA

I didn't know you were like this. I always thought you were more the sentimental kind.

NICOLAS

You know, it'd be easier if you'd help me.

LINDA

What do I have to do now?

NICOLAS

Your left leg...

Linda extends her left leg. Nicolas takes it and secures her ankle with a weaver's knot.

LINDA

Are you married?

NICOLAS

Yes.

LINDA

Your wife isn't enough for you or what?

NICOLAS

In a few days my wife and I are leaving on our honeymoon. We've been living together for about a year now and we're finally treating ourselves to a real honeymoon.

LINDA

What's your wife's name?

NICOLAS

Sylvie.

Throbbing flashes of Sylvie: her expression, hair, mouth, closed eyes, hands rubbing her breasts steadily as though to soothe them.

LINDA

Why don't you get undressed? If you were naked at least I could do what I did for Stan last night.

NICOLAS

No, I'm not getting undressed!

Nicolas is sweating; he stares at Linda, eyes bulging. Suddenly he cries out softly and grimaces in pain. He collapses onto Linda's naked body, his head on her breasts.

LINDA

Go on, stay there; it'll relax you a little. Something's wrong, I can tell.

(The dialogue isn't particularly important; it suddenly becomes confused. A slowness, impossible to define except through images, is introduced as this scene develops.)

LINDA

You know, it's almost time for rehearsal to start. You'll have to untie me...And to tell you the truth I'm shivering in this air conditioning. I've always told Stan this cold air's unhealthy.

NICOLAS

Hold on, I'll go and get something to cut the rope.

The camera follows him in medium closeup as he goes into the kitchen. He looks in several drawers. Closeup of Linda lying on the bed. She throws her head back and notices Nicolas just behind her, motionless, a pair of scissors in his left hand.

LINDA

You're left-handed!

Nicolas walks around the bed and sits down next to Linda, facing her.

NICOLAS

No, I'm not.

LINDA

But you're holding the scissors in your left hand.

NICOLAS

I know...

20

With a rapid motion Nicolas seizes Linda by the throat and strangles her. She struggles as well as she can.

LINDA

No, no, no, please...

Nicolas immediately releases his grip. Linda is breathing noisily.

NICOLAS

That's all.

Nicolas cuts the rope that was tying Linda to the bed-posts. Linda closes her eyes. They are still shut after she is untied. Nicolas takes the scissors back to the kitchen; when he returns Linda is picking up her clothes. She goes into the bathroom and comes out shortly after.

NICOLAS

Your zipper isn't done up properly. Turn around, I'll fix it.

She turns her back to Nicolas who keeps his word, conscientiously. When his hands are in Linda's hair a series of shots of Sylvie's hair are interpolated. Nicolas' face is marked with tenderness; we hear him off camera.

NICOLAS

There's rosemary, that's for remembrance. Pray you, love, remember.
And there is pansies, that's for thoughts.

Linda looks at him, subdued, mystified. Fade to black.


(The end of this scene drops off; we suddenly find ourselves at the end of a hexameter when we thought we were sailing along an alexandrine.)


Linda, fully dressed, tied to the bed. There is a roll of gauze in her mouth and she is gasping. Nicolas looks at her from very close.

NICOLAS

Promise you won't scream and I'll take that out of your mouth.

> She nods. Nicolas takes the gauze out of her mouth and throws it to the floor where the roll unwinds partially, leaving a white trail.

LINDA

Just what's going on here, Nicolas Vanesse?

NICOLAS

I don't know.

LINDA

Will it last much longer? Because in case you hadn't noticed, this position isn't very comfortable for me.

NICOLAS

Don't yell like that or I'll gag you!

LINDA

All right. You know, Nicolas, you could have just asked me instead of carrying on like that. I would have got undressed and I would have done what you wanted.

> Nicolas walks away from the bed. Medium shot of him at the window: he draws the curtains, plunging the room into semi-darkness. There is no sound but the hum of the air-conditioner.

LINDA

Why did you do that? Why?

> Nicolas slowly moves towards Linda; he sits down on the bed close to her and puts his hand on her belly. His hand slips towards her vulva and he rubs it roughly.

LINDA

Here, lie down and I'll do what I did for your friend Stan last night. Get undressed.

NICOLAS

Linda, soon I'm going to be offering you an important part in a film, my film. Shooting starts around the end of September.

LINDA

What's your film about? Can you tell me anything about it now?

NICOLAS

I could talk about it for hours, all day and all night. But I don't want to just now. In September, all right? After we've taped Hamlet I'm leaving Montreal for five or six weeks. And I'm going to finish my screenplay while I'm away.

LINDA

A holiday, eh?

NICOLAS

No, it's my honeymoon.


(As Linda's reaction is predictable, perhaps it's superfluous to show it on the screen. Certainly, though, the viewer will experience the same surprise as she. The very idea that at such a moment and in the presence of a woman whom he has tied to a bed and continues to caress inhumanly Nicolas should speak of his forthcoming honeymoon makes his character seem especially peculiar.)


Moving shot of Nicolas' hand on Linda's belly.

LINDA

A honeymoon? Did I really hear you say that?

NICOLAS

Yes.

Swish pan to Linda tied to the bed in the cabin-cruiser *Arctic* docked near the Ny Ålesund mooring-mast. The boat is empty; its hull is obedient only to the slow waves which come to the inner harbour. Day. There is hardly any activity on the docks.

LINDA

Your honeymoon...

Closeup of Linda.

Marine shot of Ny Ålesund. The *Nordnorge*, filled with passengers, is smoothly approaching the dock. Harbour activities follow: whistles blow, crowds rush to the dock, cables, gangways are lowered, passengers leave the boat. Linda, untied, is gently rubbing her ankles and wrists. She is sitting in a large armchair. Nicolas is greedily drinking from a glass of scotch.

Still shot of Ny Ålesund.

Nicolas kneels in front of the armchair; he rubs Linda's ankles slowly. All is silence. Closeup of Linda.

LINDA
No, come on, you can't! Put off your honeymoon...

But Nicolas is already in the chair with Linda and he has lifted her dress. Linda is panic-stricken, disconcerted.

LINDA
What's the matter, Nicolas? It was all right for you, wasn't it?

The lens is suddenly veiled by a piece of crumpled fabric. A few inaudible words. Cut.


(Other variations on this scene may be imagined, but their cumulative effect would still not increase the implicit force of the scenario. The characteristic of each combinatory process is to generate a growing sense of hesitation during the production. As the combinations are executed the range of possibilities closes in and the anguish of anticipated combinations begins. This very anguish contains a certain narrative suspense related to the fact that in time, the number of usable circuits is inexorably reduced. At this point in the scenario a large number of compossibles opens the film and almost immediately wipes out the fear of what is to come. The mouldings of the Nathorst, the crevasses of Cape Mitra, the glossy schists of the Beerenberg, the great doric rushes of the Chain of the Seven Glaciers, are all so many elements which keep the diaphragm stop wide open. Along the way these Archaean masses should come together with a chain of meanings, be integrated into the film which is being made and does not yet exist. It is the same for the mast at Ny Ålesund; for the moment it seems to be floating in a layer of fog, but it must become one of the identifiable components of the film. So it is appropriate to move the queen and the bishop now, and for the chess-board to cease to be an unmoving puzzle and become the effusiveness of life.)

> Apartment of Sylvie and Nicolas. Sylvie's poppy-red dress is draped over the back of an armchair; on the rug, her travelling shoes and Nile-green bag. Nicolas is putting a map into a compartment of his suitcase. With a few quick movements he slips into his trousers, puts on his shirt and knots his tie. Sylvie comes out of the bathroom and begins to get dressed and ready to leave, then goes into the bedroom, picks up a pendant and puts on the long chain to which it is attached. She examines herself in the mirror. Nicolas takes Sylvie in his arms and lifts her up; then he lets her slide along his body as he kisses her.

NICOLAS
Well, that's it, we're leaving on our honeymoon.

SYLVIE
I've got tears in my eyes, love.

> She wipes her tears in front of the mirror. Nicolas dials a number on the telephone.

NICOLAS
Taxi for 3875 Berri, apartment 1209. Vanesse. Thanks.

Exterior travelling shot. The taxi is driving at top speed towards Dorval. The speed is absolutely excessive, but Sylvie and Nicolas are relaxed and serene. They smile tenderly at one another, not saying a word, while Montreal rushes past them in a hallucinating rhythm. Medium shot of Sylvie (fish-eye lens, Nicolas' POV): Sylvie is in the right foreground, the rest of the shot is filled with enormous capital letters, which move past like a series of billboards: FORTINBRAS. After the last letter, reverse shot: Nicolas is in the left foreground: the rest of the shot reveals the beginning of an enormous latitudinal poster that depicts a naked woman lying on a board. Her eyes are closed and her hair is an extension of her body along the same horizontal plane. The oneiric velocity of the taxi in which Sylvie and Nicolas are riding can be measured by other shots through the windshield and rear-view mirror. Medium shot with Nicolas in left foreground; the landscape behind him, rather than going very fast, unfolds very slowly. The gigantic poster of the reclining woman goes past in the opposite direction, from the hair to the feet, as Nicolas smiles affectionately at Sylvie. Reverse shot: Sylvie in right foreground responds to Nicolas' loving smile in a slow fade which makes the poster-woman appear from feet to head (because the taxi has just changed direction). However, it is as though the poster has been torn at irregular intervals: some pieces are missing from the horizontal representation of the naked woman. Towards the end of this shot Sylvie, still smiling, slides across the car seat towards Nicolas. Cut.

Sudden roar of jet engines. Close shot of the cockpit of a DC-10. Under the pilot's window we can read clearly: Helsingør. High-angle long shot: the DC-10, bearing the colours of SAS, is moving slowly through the other aircraft parked around the terminal. After leaving the tarmac, the aircraft heads for the southeast end of the runway, makes a half-turn and takes off obliquely above the airport in a northwesterly direction.

Airplane. Interior. Nicolas is at the window, Sylvie in the next seat leaning over him and looking with him at the flattened view of the Montreal area. The sky-scrapers cast spots of shadow on a depressed surface with the muddy waters of the Ottawa River and Lac Saint-Louis flowing through it. Higher up, towards Verchères, we see clearly the interconnected terraces of the St. Lawrence River valley. The plane follows the river and heads towards the estuary, a suspended river. Several low-angle shots of the SAS craft; it seems to be guided by the marine beacons and landmarks of the South Shore. Interior shots: Nicolas looking down, in the distance; Sylvie is leaning against him, her blonde hair spread over his jacket. She looks around furtively to see whether the other passengers are watching them, then slips her hand inside Nicolas' trousers. Sylvie's inquisitive look as she caresses him.

NICOLAS

Yes.

SYLVIE

All the way?

NICOLAS

Yes, all the way.

SYLVIE

How long has it been?

NICOLAS

Two or three days.

Sylvie nimbly withdraws her hand. The hostess is bending over them with a menu and the wine list.

SYLVIE

What are you thinking about, love?

NICOLAS

I'm watching the river. I think we're moving away from it now. Here, come and look.

> She leans over him, lightly places one hand on his erect penis, the other on his knee; she presses her face against the window and looks out.

SYLVIE

It's as though we were looking at the river from a distance. Nicolas, am I hurting you?

NICOLAS

On the contrary; stay there; I can't tell you how good it feels.

(Find a filmic metaphor for happiness. Slanted shots of eyes or profiles shot in silhouette. It is important not to overload it, for bliss is not measured by intensity. Now that the honeymoon has begun, all is transformed. The second river flows through the soul of the couple who are trying to decipher the writing of the rivers, furrows and gaps below them. The plane trip over northern Quebec also represents, through its altitude and trajectory towards the pole, the quest for the absolute.)

> Night falls on night. There is nothing more to see; but Nicolas is still looking out as though to find some reference points, useless beacons, ghost towns, in this darkened desert. He is looking through a black window. The hostesses come back with carts laden with liqueurs, cigarettes, sumptuous objects. Nicolas sees the reflection of a hostess in the window. Suddenly everything decomposes: the sound freezes or breaks down, the lighting flickers, the words exchanged around Nicolas are retransmitted, superimposed at various speeds and cut up as though by a kind of meat-grinder.

FB: Linda is tied to the bed-posts. One detail has been changed: there is no roll of gauze in her mouth. She is beaming as though it is profoundly exciting for her to be tied up. In the foreground we see Linda's body and in the background Nicolas standing and looking at her. Linda raises the lower part of her abdomen in small thrusts, then more deliberately; she closes her eyes, miming with a wealth of details the pleasure which has just reached a peak in this coitus with an imaginary being. Closeup of Nicolas near the bed. We hear Linda panting and her blissful sighs. Nicholas takes off his clothes with immoderate eagerness.

LINDA

What are you doing? You're taking too long. Come on, hurry.

Medium shot of a hostess bending over Nicolas.

HOSTESS

Something else, sir?

NICOLAS

An Aquavit, please.

HOSTESS

I notice that Madame is asleep...Shall I bring a blanket for her?

NICOLAS

No, thank you.

After the medium shot of the hostess, cut to a shot of Nicolas getting undressed. These shots should follow one another rapidly. Linda is moaning, her eyes closed; Nicolas gets on top of her. Closeup of Nicolas, his tense features suddenly relaxing. Then, in great visual confusion, Nicolas' hoarse groaning. Cut.

Nicolas swallows his Aquavit in one gulp. He looks around him. Everything is peaceful now; the night-lights have been turned on, transforming the cabin of

the airplane into a restful cavern. Sylvie emerges from
her half-sleep.

SYLVIE

I was asleep.

NICOLAS

Just for a bit.

SYLVIE

Don't you feel tired?

Nicolas unfolds the map showing the SAS transatlantic
flight paths. Sylvie consults it with him. We can discern
the yellow mass of the Canadian Shield and the long
blue lines going from Chicago and New York to the
North Pole.

SYLVIE

Where are we now?

NICOLAS

Just about there... We'll be over the ocean soon.

(Sylvie and Nicolas kiss as though discovering each other for
the first time. In fact they *are* rediscovering each other for the
very first time, caressing each other in the aircraft transport-
ing them above the frozen landscape of the sub-polar night,
beyond the country's boundaries. Their motions, infinitely
slow, resemble those they would perform in bed, yet they are
not in a celestial bed but on a flying raft with people crowded
inside it. In their own eyes they are naked; love is enfolding
them in a nebulous fabric. They hear a murmur around them,
voices, presences, but all that matters now is the intimate
sound the lovers hear: the bursting of schemes, the shared
impetus overlapping the large hole the airplane makes in the
black space, a symphony of hope and desire.)

Nicolas puts his arms around Sylvie, who has fallen
asleep against him. He holds her so as not to disturb her

sleep, for she is breathing deeply now and slipping further and further into the depths of herself. Nicolas holds Sylvie like a child who has fallen asleep during a long trip. As Nicolas raises his right hand to place it just below Sylvie's breasts she moves slightly and her silver pendant drops onto his hand. Closeup: Nicolas does not look down. The camera shows the movement of the object which is superimposed on Nicolas' caress.

Very tight closeup of the pendant. The object is circular and represents nothing but the counter-image of a convex plexus with numerous bars that join the eruptive and ambiguous core to its crown. Closeup of Nicolas looking down at the piece of jewellery, which is on the back of his right hand. Zoom in on the pendant.

Dissolve to the pendant stained with blood. Nicolas staring into space; his face darkens. The image is fragmented in numerous frames which disappear one at a time to reveal the bedroom in Sylvie and Nicolas' apartment. Sylvie is on the bed, very stiff, her features hardened.

SYLVIE
Why do you want to know his name?

NICOLAS
What difference does it make? I want to know.

SYLVIE
And if I beg you not to ask me?

NICOLAS
What's in a name? It's not a name that's made me suffer.

SYLVIE
A name isn't something you can say.

NICOLAS
Why not?

SYLVIE

A name is sacred. You just don't say it!

NICOLAS

If you don't tell me his name I'll hit you!

> Nicolas sits in a chair and waits. Sylvie is tormented, reluctant; she lets the silence last as long as she thinks it possible. Then she recites rapidly:

SYLVIE

Michel Lewandowski. He's 49; married, two children, both girls. Profession: financial advisor. Grey hair. His address and phone number are in the book. Nicolas, I committed a grave fault and I beg you to forgive me.

NICOLAS

It's done; you know very well that I forgive you.

SYLVIE

Why did you insist on knowing his name?

NICOLAS

Because as you say, a name is sacred...and...I don't know, Sylvie, I don't know.

> Nicolas goes to Sylvie, takes her in his arms, holding her head against his bare chest. He embraces her, caressing her very solicitously. Suddenly she turns towards him and unfastens her dressing gown; with a few abrupt movements she strips naked and lies on the bed, the back of her neck propped against the pillow, her eyes blank.

(Duration prevails forever over modes of succession. What follows is already divided, keeps subdividing *ad vertiginem*, whereas what endures is one, monadic and indivisible. In the screenplay nothing needs to last, everything follows and is cut by the stopwatch. The temporal flow is fragmented by a series of frames and under the pressure of this metamorphosis the sustained, gradual development is reduced to a sequence of sequences, a vivid ash. The sequences do more than follow one another: they are tangled, superimposed, they copenetrate, respond to one another and divide in a parody of temporal flow. Time flies, no doubt... When we speak of time it has already passed; only dead images of it remain. Cinematographic cutting only accentuates the obliterated nature of time; the film decomposes indefinitely that which is already complete. But beginning with these fragments, still more or less attached to the outpourings from which they come, the spectator can reconstitute the power of the primal energy of time. Thus the extreme discontinuity serves as a springboard that enables the spectator to reinvent the contexture of original time. When this operation is over the spectator will come back from a multitude of successions to the duration which underlies them all, and he will experience from within a single intoxicating duration. Time thus captivated loses a little of its volatile elusive appearance. Time reinvented from its own microliths continues its gradual development; it keeps spreading and extending through the viewer's secret experience.)

Sylvie and Nicolas' apartment. Bedroom. In the shadows we can distinguish the naked bodies of Sylvie and Nicolas. Swish pan to Sylvie's pendant on the bedside table. She lets out a series of shouts, each different from the preceding one, the whole constituting an exalted plainsong.

NICOLAS
Sylvie, what are you doing?!!! Don't move away like that, I'm coming...

Sylvie's hand slips onto the bedside table, winds around her wrist the chain that holds the pendant. The camera pulls back quickly and takes an establishing shot of the bed. Sylvie has one knee on the bed and she bends over Nicolas just as he is ejaculating, with a moan. Sylvie strikes Nicolas violently with the pendant, swinging it from the end of the chain. The first blow hits Nicolas in the back, because he turned around as he was ejaculating. He yells with pain, then turns towards Sylvie, dismayed, but the pendant has just struck his abdomen. Sylvie is completely unleashed.

NICOLAS

Sylvie, no, no, don't do that!

Sylvie is weeping bitterly, as though terror-stricken. All her softness has been abruptly transformed into a sort of blind rage. Nicolas is still on the bed. With a lightning motion Sylvie strikes him, aiming at his groin. He lets out a cry of horror as he feels blood flowing from his penis onto his thighs and hands. Cut.

Airplane. Interior. Medium shot: Sylvie is curled up on the seat, her blonde head on Nicolas' lap. On Nicolas' thigh, the pendant. We can easily make out the hyacinth of Compostello which is the dark heart of this monstrance. Nicolas succumbs to sleep, as though fascinated by the communicating cavities in the pendant. He lowers his eyes. Cut.

(A succession is never finished. When it is transmitted the following ineluctable operation is attached to it: another succession. And this continues, is reproduced, begins again, stops just long enough to begin yet again and so on. What follows is finally, inevitably, obsessive. No one is immune to the dissolution of time. Even sleep has never dammed up the savage waters of remembrance.)

Sylvie and Nicolas' bedroom, the same night. Nicolas has collapsed on the bed, naked, while Sylvie, still wearing her underpants and brassiere, is arched over him. It is necessary to understand – without seeing too much, of course – that Sylvie is fellating him. Through Nicolas' passivity, the labial sounds, Sylvie's wordless application, the spectator guesses at the precise nature of their amorous relations. Closeup of Nicolas: his eyelids are so low it seems as though he is looking towards the inside of his skull; his breathing is deep and vibrant like a volcano before the lava flows from its lake of fire. The *cursus fellationis* proceeds, its thrust is maintained. Nicolas is possessed; one might even believe that he is being levitated, that Sylvie's sibilant mouth is all that keeps him down on the bed. When Nicolas' moans change to stridulations the screen becomes extra-luminous. Overexposed shots of the couple taken from various angles; single closing shot: Sylvie lifts up her hair and stands by the bed. She wipes her lips. Nicolas grabs her by the wrist and drags her forcibly to make her finish what she has started. She resists as well as she can, but falls on top of him as they struggle. Nicolas immediately clutches her by the hair to be sure that she stays on him. She quickly frees herself, snatches the pendant from the bedside table and strikes Nicolas with great violence. The image now becomes so overexposed that it is difficult to discern anything but silhouettes. The sound goes on, however, until the blackout.

Ambient sound of the inside of the airplane. Sylvie and Nicolas are still asleep, close together on the seat.

Nicolas is sitting on the edge of the bed, throwing blood-soaked pads onto the rug. There are already several on the floor. Nicolas keeps applying them and does not take his eyes off his penis between two pads. The camera pulls back quickly and shows us Nicolas sitting naked on the seat in the airplane; there is a small pile of soiled pads beside Sylvie. A hostess walks past Nicolas without turning her head. Fade to black.

Sylvie and Nicolas' apartment, the same night. Sylvie, in tears, is getting dressed, very close to Nicolas who is prostrate on the bed and busy tending his wound. Sylvie must be very closely described by the camera in the shots which follow: they will constitute the first icon of Sylvie Dubuque. She dresses in front of the camera, as though the lens were a mirror. She puts on her madder-red dress with wide pleats and a border of Chantilly lace. Sylvie's complexion is very pale, her hair and eye-lashes blonde – a sensuous blonde whose warm and regular pigmentation attests to the authenticity of the colour. Her large eyes seem lost, for Sylvie is visibly moved by what has just happened between her and Nicolas. Her pupils can barely be distinguished from the irises, which are nearly black. Her well-drawn lips, swollen, the perfect wings of her nose, her broad forehead, everything about her face is in harmony with her body, which is all delicacy and beauty.

(Describing this sequence in words verges on the impossible. The filmic image can barely be represented in writing. When a certain number of anthropometric details about Sylvie have been listed, the result resembles a plaster mould more than a representation of something that can move. Writing spoils the movement of life, whereas the cinema, less precise at description, renders what is most precious about those whom it represents: movement. Sylvie is first and foremost a warm and charming presence. A thin lachrymal film covers her eyes and confers on them not only a kind of moist adherence to reality but also a tragic quality which is becoming to her whole person. Sylvie has been crying or is about to start cry-ing: yes, she goes through life with wet eyes, masked, in a way, by a transparent secretion. Her expression, even more than her other corporeal properties, epitomizes her: it is in-tense, marked by anguish and passion. Her expression, con-stantly shifting, is what most connects her to the invisible. But how to give a precise idea of her body? Invoking Titian or Tiepolo is a reference to fixed images. And yet these points of reference are not completely ineffectual, for a halo of splendour suffuses Tiepolo's air-borne women. Is it not the same for Sylvie? Sumptuous, captivating (her rather broken voice only adds to this quality), embodied with a connotation of plenitude, unvarying in her attractive force, Sylvie is the ultimate woman, the mirror of love, the hollow vessel of Snaebjørn, the work of works. From the beginning – and for some time yet to come – Sylvie is the bearing structure of the film: everything refers to her, is grafted to her skin, everything is measured in terms of her. She is the beginning and the end of all the sequences, and the allusive symbol of duration.)

> Airplane. Interior. Nicolas is waking up; he looks out the window. Below, an enormous liquid carpet, nothing more. Nicolas takes his toilet kit from the suitcase under his seat. Sylvie mutters something as he moves, but doesn't even open her eyes; she stays asleep. Nicolas goes to the washroom.

> Zoom-back: Sylvie, in underpants and brassiere, moves away from the bed, holding the blood-stained pendant. She looks at the pendant and drops it. She walks away, puts on her madder-red dress, looking at herself in the lens of the camera. Tears are streaming down her cheeks. She takes long pauses, looking at Nicolas. She picks up her bag and leaves the apartment.

> Closeup of Nicolas in the airplane washroom: he is shaving. He looks very closely at himself in the mirror, makes some faces – this seems to be an obsession of his.

> Shot of Sylvie leaning over to look out the window. As she looks she is so absorbed in her contemplation that she does not even notice Nicolas' return. He approaches her and kisses her neck.

SYLVIE
Look, Nicolas. We're flying over Norway, I think.

Shots of the couple in silhouette: their profiles are incandescent on an incandescent ground. Activity resumes on board the plane: passengers are awakened, breakfast is served, announcements in Norwegian come over the loudspeakers. Traffic in the aisles has become heavy again.

SYLVIE

The landscape looks impressive from up here. I can make out the cliffs; I can see enormous white surfaces, glaciers maybe.

NICOLAS

I think you're right, Sylvie. They do look like glaciers. Here, sit on my lap; we can look together.

Sylvie sits on Nicolas' lap, her right arm around his neck.

NICOLAS

When you see them from this height the massifs don't seem to have any relief, or very little. The summits look like pin heads, the glaciers are like snowflakes with dark rings around them.

SYLVIE

Look, Nicolas, look over here.

But he is lost in his internal reverie: he does not hear Sylvie.

NICOLAS

Sylvie, I don't know why, but I suddenly feel sick at heart.


(Discontinuity presupposes continuity. This applies to the series of lines in a dialogue as well as to the very substructure of the film. "Heartsick," in this case, represents continuity, while the sentences that preceded are circuit-breakers. We describe as discontinuous that which transgresses logical continuity in temporal order, according to a preconceived plan. Even if our idea of time takes in certain divergences in speed or even deviations, the fact remains that we consider to be discontinuous anything that refers to unpredictable breaks or extensions. For what is predictable develops only in the serenity of reason. Continuity is a sequence without ellipses, leaps or jolts, without cuts or lateral excursus. In the eyes of memory, existence sometimes has this abnormally continuous quality, and so the most discordant elements fit together through an effect of perspective, according to the purest linearity. In fact, the course of life is chaotic and unpredictable. No fiction can mask the unpredictable "order" of existence. The unpredictable, apparently, contains the basal formulae of all factitious representations of life. Actual experiences do not follow logically to form an essence that endures while it comes increasingly to resemble its own image. No, temporal flow is an impure torrent whose fluid violence transports the unpredictable existence that develops as the matrical water descends towards a valley, any valley at all. This torrential fall defines life better than all the solid elements that are carried along in its course. The discontinuity of the film is only the formal face of the discontinuity of all that lives. A demonstration of this prolepsis would require a certain discursive continuity, a proof of movement beginning with immobility or the vital torrent beginning with the rocks that it transports. A certain ellipse must occur by itself, then, when it comes to perceiving the flowing specificity of life, so that the viewer, scatter-brained and sometimes agitated, can find the path of the torrent by himself.)

Kisses follow Nicolas' confession: Sylvie's long kisses, filled with softness and desire. The captain's voice can be heard over the loudspeakers. At the same time the DC-10 turns above Hurumlandet and the Nesodden peninsula, makes a series of corrections and then lines up with the runway. Passengers are looking out on both sides of the plane. The islands of the Bundefjord and the Oslofjord break away from the wings of the plane to form green crystals in the blueish water. Then come the

Fornebu peninsula, the first approach beacons, and waiting.

Exterior. A DC-10 is approaching the landing-strip at Fornebu. It lands smoothly. Instead of following the plane the camera pivots and stops on a frame in which we can see Oslo at the end of the fjord.

Eva Vos, a young woman around 25, leaves an apartment building located at Jan Mayenplassen, 79, in Holmen, a suburb northwest of Oslo. She is wearing a gold and white suit: slacks, jacket, foulard. She gets behind the wheel of a Renault 15 and heads south. She drives onto the Holmenkollveien, a fairly congested highway. It is 8:45 a.m. After a few minutes of bumper-to-bumper traffic Eva Vos takes the Ullernchausseen, heading southwest. Eva is going to Marienlyst where the offices and studios of the state radio and television network – the NRK – are concentrated. Dissolve: Eva Vos goes into the main NRK building. Immediately a receptionist calls to her; Eva Vos and the receptionist exchange a few words. Eva runs back outside. In the parking lot she handles her R15 skilfully. She exits onto the E18 and drives at full speed. Dissolve: Eva's car driving into the parking area at the Fornebu airport.

(For the spectator, Eva Vos's appearance is more disconcerting than mystifying. She gives the impression of having been parachuted completely unexpectedly into the plot. Eva qualifies as an intruder in this world where she has not been subtly inserted.)

A porter is pushing a luggage-carrier with all the suitcases piled on it. A crowd is rushing out of customs.

Eva

Sylvie!

Sylvie turns around, sees Eva coming up to her all smiles. The two women embrace warmly.

SYLVIE

Eva, this is my husband, Nicolas Vanesse.

NICOLAS

Sylvie's told me a lot about you.

> The camera trucks on a crab dolly and cranes up. Travelling shot to the airport exit. Stay on high-angle long shot: we see Eva walking away, going to get her R15, coming back, etc. Dissolve: Eva driving Sylvie and Nicolas.

EVA

Your plane was a good hour early. It's a miracle I got to the airport on time...My secretary had the brilliant idea of checking with SAS.

> Closeup: Nicolas is looking at everything, to the point of absent-mindedness: the landscape, houses, people, the highway. As they approach the city on the raised highway, Nicolas sees the fjord, the islands, the docks of Oslo and the city spread over the hills. He would like to stop in a field, any field, but stop, yes, stop, before going into Oslo, before crossing the official limits of Oslo. But Eva Vos is driving at a steady speed and the car is going through the streets of Oslo. Nicolas suddenly closes his eyes as though succumbing to sleep. An image is superimposed on his face. We see, on a stage set up in a field, a company of actors declaiming, moving, gesticulating with strange solemnity. Swish pan from this image to a travelling shot in a taxi going towards Dorval just as the name Fortinbras is moving past.

> Eva stops the car in front of the Fønix Hotel. A porter rushes over to take the suitcases.

EVA

Bye, see you tonight.

SYLVIE

What is it, love? You look sad.

NICOLAS

No, Sylvie, I'm tired.

> Dissolve: sixth floor of the Fønix Hotel. Sylvie and
> Nicolas are following the porter. Sylvie is the first to go
> into room 608. Another dissolve: the porter leaves the
> room, closing door number 608. The camera stays in the
> hallway. Still shot of the door.

> Superimposed on the closed door, a low-angle shot of
> the Newtontoppen, covered with ice and snow, hostile,
> wild; then, still in superimposition on door number 608,
> a series of shots of the Paulabreen glacier. After the
> superimpositions, focus on the closed door. Keep the
> same frame line from beginning to end. Cut.

> Terrace of the Pernille Restaurant, on Karljohansgate.
> The meal is finished. Nicolas gets up from the table and
> goes to the washroom.

EVA

Tell me about your husband: did you know him when I was
in Montreal last year?

SYLVIE

Just slightly, I think...

EVA

Does he know Michel?

SYLVIE

Don't ever mention Michel's name in front of Nic, I beg you.

EVA

Don't worry. You know, I can tell you now, I was jealous of
you in Montreal...because of Michel.

SYLVIE

You like him?

EVA

I thought he was very handsome and charming...Is it painful
for you when I talk about him? I'm an idiot. Oh, I'm angry at

myself. Please forget it, Sylvie, and forgive me for being so tactless.

SYLVIE

I'm not annoyed at you, Eva.

Sylvie takes Eva's hand affectionately and brings it to her lips so suddenly that they are both disturbed by it.

EVA

Are you happy with Nicolas?

SYLVIE

Yes, I will be happy. Doesn't it show a little in the way I look?

EVA

When I saw you at Fornebu I thought you looked superb, really...It makes me so happy to see you again.

SYLVIE

You finally decided not to bleach your hair blonde?

EVA

I prefer to stay brunette; it's more original in Norway.

SYLVIE

You're talking nonsense for the tourists!

EVA

I met a man about six months ago. It was a disaster, so I went back to my solitary life. I pay dearly for love, with depressions. I don't know why...I'm no uglier than the next person.

SYLVIE

What are you talking about? You're beautiful!

EVA

Nothing's happening.

Nicolas comes back to the table. Eva and Sylvie have already stopped talking.

NICOLAS

What's going on? This isn't the time to recite the *Benedicite*, we've finished eating. But Eva, I'll talk to you: ask the waiter for three double Aquavits.

> Eva gestures to the waiter and gives him the order. At the same moment, Sylvie gets up and kisses Nicolas on the mouth with great passion.

SYLVIE

So you'll know I love you!

NICOLAS

It's very mild tonight, almost warm.

EVA

I have to tell you...A while ago we were talking about Fortinbras. And I think I've confused Rosenkrantz and Fortinbras...

NICOLAS

Is there a Fortinbras Street in Oslo?

EVA

I don't know. In a monarchy every prince is entitled to his own street or public park. I don't know Oslo as well as people who were born here: when I left Stavanger where I was born and moved here, I was already 21. Tell me, how does Fortinbras die in Shakespeare's play?

NICOLAS

Fortinbras doesn't die.

EVA

Another ghost?

NICOLAS

Much worse: someone who doesn't die. An obsession...

EVA

In every town in Norway there's a Rosenkrantzgate. Maybe Rosenkrantz has more meaning for Norway than Fortinbras, no?

NICOLAS

Rosenkrantz is a Dane; I don't understand.

SYLVIE

You've never told me about all that, Nicolas...Fortinbras, Prince of Norway, Hamlet, Prince of Denmark. I didn't know about that parallel. It's fascinating. I've got the feeling that you just have to line up the names and profound new realities will instantly develop.

NICOLAS

I think just the opposite, love. Names don't give birth to subterranean meanings; that would be tantamount to a purely literary process – anti-cinematographic, you know! Designations of reality add nothing to reality, except a nominal mask. And when you get right down to it, I think subterranean meanings are completely secondary. I'd rather think in terms of extensions in space and time instead of giving the basement more significant value simply because it supports the other levels of reality that aren't so dense. In the cinema we start right off with an unnamed reality; we exhaust it on the surface, run through it, fly over it, explore it – without ever going below the line of the horizon. We don't even have to go into it deeply. Perhaps we don't even have to name it. I'm more and more inclined to think that nominal reality is a world that's finished. We don't live in a verbal universe any more, we live in the crystalline lens of our eyes.

SYLVIE

Names aren't sacred any more.

> Dolly out: the group is very far from the camera but still discernible on the illuminated terrace of the Pernille. As we dolly out, the visual field enlarges, moving the camera lens away from the group at the table. The camera makes a quarter-turn: we see the fjord, a few illuminated boats, then another quarter-turn towards the east. Establishing shot of the Storting; in the left foreground, a plaque attached to a street-light on which we can read distinctly: Rosenkrantzgate. Cut.

> The airport at Trondheim. Sylvie and Nicolas are sitting in the bar, at the big window that looks down on the

tarmac. The Wideroe Flyselskab Fairchild F44 is being fueled as they look on; Sylvie is drinking coffee, Nicolas a Bokkøl beer. A message begins to crackle out of the loudspeaker in the bar; Sylvie and Nicolas get out of their chairs and go hand in hand towards the exit on the ground floor.

SYLVIE

Do you love me?

NICOLAS

Yes, I love you.

SYLVIE

How long is it from here to Tromsø?

NICOLAS

Almost two hours.

The passengers get into the plane.

Dissolve: the airplane taxis to the end of the runway and takes off. From an elevated point of view: we see the plane fly over the second-last bend of the Nidelva, then the fortress of Kristiansten and the memory city of Nidaros, a northern Christian metropolis and residence of the ancient kings of Norway. The plane modifies its course and heads north. The camera comes back down towards the ground; and at this moment the viewer understands that there has been a change in point of view, because we see Nicolas coming out of the Linnea Hotel wearing a sweater. From the top of the hotel steps he watches the traffic on Sondregate. Hands in his pockets, he steps onto the sidewalk, observing the crowd of passersby as he walks among them. The streets of the old city are broad, inordinately spacious, conferring on the Nidaros peninsula a solemn beauty that seems unchangeable. Nicolas walks to the Fjordgaten where the cool wind heralds September. He walks beside the water, looking haggard, rather sad. He leans against a low wall, looks at the fjord, goes away, visibly not knowing what to do with his time. He comes back to the centre of town, along Nordregate. Travelling shot. He goes into a café, sits at a table, orders a Bokkøl and drinks it as he flips through the London *Times* which is there for the customers, rolled around a wooden rod like a crêpe.

(Something's wrong here. If Nicolas is flipping through the *Times* it means that time can only be retrospective. Now time, perennial and never killed, circulates like the fluid, ghostly mass that is squeezing Nidaros and climbing, descending, climbing again up the docks, following the series of waves from the Sea of Norway, which enter the fjords from the west. This last sequence in Trondheim is presented like a dark, fathomless cavity. One does not flip through time, rather it is time that invades everything, a morbid percolation, which nothing combats, and which transforms all joy into its nostalgia and all love into despair. Find a drifting form like the solitary and inexplicable drift of Nicolas Vanesse in this ancient capital at the mouth of the Nidelva.)

The day is slowly tipping over. The streets of Trondheim are filled with its large population going in every direction. Nicolas Vanesse, looking dreamy, is following shadows, contemplating façades that are Hanseatic vestiges, fragments of the ever-darkening sky. He stops before the window of a watchmaker's shop: all the clocks and time-pieces have stopped. Cut.

(A touch of Caligarism, an overly expressive insignificance: time, like Nicolas, has rings around its eyes.)

The Wideroe Flyselskab Fairchild F-44 comes to a final stop in front of the Tromsø airport. The passengers get out. Sylvie and Nicolas seem lost in this distant post almost at the tip of the Scandinavian shield.

SYLVIE

You know, Nicolas, I'm really enjoying this trip. I love you. You're my whole life, my love.

NICOLAS

Ever since we've been in Norway (but it hasn't even been three days yet) I've felt relaxed. Really, our honeymoon is marvellous. During the last few weeks before we left Montreal I felt disheartened; nothing was going right. But these last few days I've really developed an appetite for life again. Last night at the Fønix when I was falling asleep I told myself that some disaster was going to happen that would keep us in Norway...and deep down inside I was delighted at the prospect.

> Nicolas arranges the suitcases that have come off the plane. He stays near the glass door through which he can see the bumpy landscape going down to the sea. There is something extreme about this panorama: it is like an infra-land, stripped bare, cut up by the fjords, haunted by the nearby North Pole.

> The taxi arrives. Nicolas gets into the garnet-coloured Volvo. Shots of the inside of the taxi. Sylvie and Nicolas looking at the abraded knolls that form a cirque around Tromsø, a city spread out along its wharves. Tromsø is a city without a centre, a long landing-stage rimmed with a few houses and buildings. As the taxi approaches Tromsø we can make out the fleet of boats and tramp steamers moored all along the ribbon of wharves. Midway between the two ends of the city a few taller buildings and an impressive haze dominate the landscape.

SYLVIE

The *Nordnorge*, likely...

> Dissolve: the red stain of the taxi bursts into the place where the *Nordnorge* is moored, with all its lights on.

There is great activity around the luxurious streamlined ship. Two bridges link it to the Elling Carlsen wharf.

Dissolve: cabin number 9 is in a corner on the second deck. It is spacious, luxurious even, and the walls are covered with maps of northern Norway and the islands. Sylvie and Nicolas come out of the cabin and go down the bridge. They set off for a stroll, hand in hand, before the *Nordnorge* leaves. Tromsø is built up on an island embedded in a landscape that contains nothing but sky. To the south we can see distant mountains. The powdery peak of the Haeggevarre emerges above the multitude of spurs between it and the Lyngseidet.

Series of shots which overlap one another by super-imposition carried out according to an unvarying scale of ⅜. Nicolas holds Sylvie's hand as he leads her along the wharves. Other shots: Sylvie stops in front of a maternity shop: expandable dresses, a Lapp back-harness for carrying babies, clothes for the newborn, cradles.

NICOLAS
You know, I was deeply hurt by that...episode with Michel Lewandowski. It destroyed me inside.

SYLVIE
I know, I know.

She moves away from the shop window.

NICOLAS
You despised me.

SYLVIE
Yes.

NICOLAS
And now?

SYLVIE
I love you, Nicolas, I love you. Don't say crazy things...

Dissolve: Sylvie is leaning on the parapet, her back to the sea, looking at the mountains that obstruct the horizon to the southeast.

NICOLAS

Sør Kvaløy or Rinvassøy – I don't know...

SYLVIE

What are you talking about?

NICOLAS

I'm trying to remember the name of the island we'll be sailing beside in a while. Sør Kvaløy, that's it, I think. Anyway, what difference does it make?

Another shot: Sylvie and Nicolas walking towards the *Nordnorge*, arms around each other's waist. Travelling shot: the camera shoots them from behind. They are not speaking but we can hear dialogue.

SYLVIE

If I were pregnant when we get back to Montreal...

NICOLAS

You're only twenty-two, love, you've still got lots of time.

SYLVIE

Of course.

NICOLAS

Childhood is so sad.

They kiss for a long time, standing at the entry to the Elling Carlsen wharf. The boat whistle sounds. End of the series of shots in Tromsø.

The ship moves rapidly away from Tromsø. It is reduced to a string of lights demarcating the water from the mountains, which seem to be piled up right on the island of Tromsø; the remote perspective condenses points that in reality are well out of phase, into a single shot. Sylvie and Nicolas are leaning on the rail.

NICOLAS

Sør Kvaløy, that's the name of the island.

SYLVIE

It looks uninhabited.

NICOLAS

Probably. We still have two more islands on our right, then we head due north.

SYLVIE

It's getting dark; I wonder if we'll be able to see them.

NICOLAS

Don't worry, you'll see them. When you're this close to the North Pole in summertime the light seeps deep into the night. Beginning now there's no more night for us.


(Here begins the *tempus continuatum* of ancient Thule. Will the viewer feel as though he is climbing the curved roof of the earth? Perhaps...In any event, like Nicolas and Sylvie who are gripping the railing of the *Nordnorge*, he must experience the dizziness of the person who moves away from the measure of time, and makes his entrance into an exhilarating instantaneity. Time does not stop, no! Time will never stop again; through the void, it suppresses everything that preceded it and everything that will follow it. We are not even aware now of the passage from one day to the next. North of Tromsø and from this moment in the film, even the eternal return seems inconceivable. A certain distortion of eternity is substituted for the nycthemeral plan. A film generally offers the viewer something like a second memory, more diversified than his own, broader, with a system of recollection the same as that of individual memory. Nothing now resembles memory except the parade of images across the giant screen. If we leave this familiar ground how can we lead the viewer to Thule, initiate him into a night which is not black, make him imagine that the repetitive definition of time is not the only one and that beyond Tromsø and Sør Kvaløy, in summertime, the counter-melody of diurnal and nocturnal is crumbling? Understanding takes time. But the viewer has already invested the characters with his own emotions; he has taken the *Nordnorge* with Sylvie and Nicolas. He is travelling with them towards a destination which he does not know, but he is preparing to discover it along with the newlyweds. The viewer finds himself in nothing less than the fetal position, borne by the film he is looking at or by the characters; what happens to the bearing person touches him, what feeds his genitor intoxicates him, what enlightens him dazzles the viewer too. Polar temporality becomes the viewer's punctiform time. Paradoxically, this continuous time, far from resembling itself and going on to induce monotony, appears to be infinitely dissimilar to itself.)

After the ship crosses the Tromsø Sund and brushes against the large island of Rinvassøy, it enters the Sea of Norway. At 8:30 p.m. the sun is still shining. It gives the impression of flying low, towards the north. But it is still shining. It isn't exactly the same sun or exactly the same light as one approaches the summit of the planet, but there is only one sun and this is it. Change lenses inside the shots – the way you spin the cylinder of a revolver – and take many shots which, by building up, can only demonstrate that no auxiliary lighting is being showered on the characters or objects within the field. This is not a white night, but a night filled with sun, well and truly filled with sun, penetrated everywhere by some intruder, raped by the light, and so producing the marriage of day and night.

Sylvie is snuggling in Nicolas' arms. The sun moves slowly in the sky, then suddenly, at 10:30 p.m., it stops above the horizon and the distance separating the disc from the ocean remains constant. It is not yet midnight, but it will never be midnight. The sun is fixed, superimposed on Sylvie's pupils, before it begins its new tra-

jectory whose vastness will subside only to rise again
after going twice around the clock.

                        NICOLAS
Aren't you cold?

                        SYLVIE
No I'm fine. I've had tears in my eyes for several minutes.

                        NICOLAS
Why, love?

                        SYLVIE
Because I'm so absolutely happy, because suddenly everything is marvellous...Let me cry a little, love.

                        NICOLAS
There's nothing around us but the sea; we're already far
away from the continent.

                        SYLVIE
Is it very far to Ny Ålesund?

                        NICOLAS
580 sea miles from Tromsø, or more than 700 land miles.

                        SYLVIE
The closer we get to the Pole, the more I'm moved.

Sylvie wipes her tears; the wind blowing off the sea is
cooler. But it is not an evening wind, even at 11:00 p.m.,
rather it is the wind from the Arctic Ocean. The evening
is completely suffused with sun and the air is as mild as
it can be at this time of year, in this sea with no shores.
The sun still hangs above the land, like the beacon that
guided Bjarni for nine times nine nights.

Dissolve: cabin 9. The cabin is plunged into a highly
relative darkness. Sylvie comes out of the bathroom,
streaming wet. She goes to the porthole which looks out
on the prow of the ship; she moves the curtain aside
slightly.

NICOLAS

If you leave the curtain open it will be light all night.

SYLVIE

But I want to see you so I can kiss you better.

NICOLAS

I like your hair up in a chignon the way you've got it now.

SYLVIE

I know why too, because you're going to take it down...

> Medium shot of the couple who embrace and roll together several times. Nicolas tries to undo Sylvie's hair while she is on top of him, caressing him with both hands.

NICOLAS

Not too much, not too much, love.

SYLVIE

Is it still sensitive? Did I hurt you?

NICOLAS

I'm afraid I'll come like that. And I want to be inside you, Sylvie. Stay on top of me.

> Sylvie straddles Nicolas, who has placed his hands on the breasts of his love. Sylvie, sea creature swayed by the moon, is rocked and lets herself be rocked by Nicolas. She is the sailor, he the sea, but he is the sailor too and she the inverted sea, the unfathomable, surging opacity that carries the *Nordnorge* along on this infinite day which began in Tromsø, or rather just north of Tromsø, in the middle of the Sea of Norway.

SYLVIE

It feels so soft inside me.

NICOLAS

You're beautiful, Sylvie, infinitely beautiful...

SYLVIE

Oh, you!...Keep pushing inside me, go on, yes, push, deeper, farther...Can you?

> Parallel travelling shot. The camera is at the head of the bed. Within its range there is Sylvie, seen from the front, and Nicolas under her. Above Sylvie's hair, now undone, we can make out the source of the light. Sylvie is back-lit. End on this frame and before the couple's double orgasm. Cut.

> Swish pan to the door of the cabin, which is opening: Nicolas appears in the doorway. He sees Sylvie lying curled up on the bed and wearing her ivy-red sweater, her nacarat slacks; she is asleep. Nicolas approaches the bed, looks at her. Several flashes of Linda Noble tied to the bed are superimposed on the image of the sleeping Sylvie. Closeup of Nicolas: he looks disturbed, undergoes a metamorphosis before the lens. He gently touches the back of Sylvie's neck and moves it slightly. Sylvie moans, turns over so that she is lying on her stomach. Nicolas slips his hand under Sylvie's sweater, all the while watching her slowly come out of her sleep.

NICOLAS

Wake up, Sylvie, we're coming to Bjørnia.

> Sylvie, eyes wide open, looks at the cabin bathed in light, Nicolas close to her.

NICOLAS

You know, the island at the south of the Barents Sea.

> They go out, hand in hand, immediately startled by the explosion of light when Nicolas opens the door. Cut.

> The next shots are taken in the back seat of a Ford Torino parked in an alley off Parc Lafontaine in Montreal. Night. The man is being forced to lie down on the seat by a girl who is obviously on drugs.

GIRL

GIRL

I pay off my debts however I can.

> The scene that follows is very violent: the girl throws
> herself on her partner. Their revels seem more like sav-
> age combat. A brief moan escapes from the man. The
> girl, still in the shadows, spits onto the floor of the car
> the sperm she has in her mouth. We can distinguish
> only her body, cut off at the shoulders by the line of the
> roof of the car (she is standing beside it). She slams the
> door, then sticks her head inside the window.

GIRL

You know, I don't even remember your name.

NICOLAS

Nicolas Vanesse.

> The girl staggers away from the car. Screams can be
> heard at the same time as the sound of the door that
> slams as it strikes against a garbage can, then Nicolas'
> retching as he vomits onto the road. Cut.

> Shots of the door of cabin 9 on the Nordnorge when the
> metal panel opens onto a pool of light.

> The Ford Torino is driving along the Bonaventure ex-
> pressway in Montreal. Nicolas is at the wheel; Sylvie is
> beside him, tense, excited, victim of a kind of internal
> rage which is consuming her. Nicolas turns on the radio
> as he drives. The noise from the radio only adds to
> Sylvie's feverish excitement. She hits Nicolas' right
> hand with her purse; she hits him repeatedly, senseless-
> ly. Nicolas raises his arm to protect his face, but she
> keeps trying to hit him. Then the contents of her purse
> spill into the car; she drops the purse to her feet. In a
> lightning motion she clambers over the seat and crum-
> ples, prostrate, onto the back seat. The car is caught in a
> stream of cars that is becoming a traffic jam. Sylvie is flat
> on her stomach passionately kissing the seat, scratching
> at it with her fingernails. The radio is still blaring, dis-

cordant music distorted by interference. Nicolas manages, with some difficulty, to get out of the stream of cars and finally stops near the administrative building of the Port of Montreal. He turns off the ignition, gets out of the car and opens the other door. He picks up Sylvie's purse, puts one of the rings of the strap back into the loop from which it has become detached. He succeeds after several attempts. Sylvie does not move. Nicolas bends over and picks up everything that has fallen out of the purse. He keeps finding things as far as the brake pedal. He puts everything back in the purse. All this happens on the well-tended lawn of the port authority. Sylvie gets out of the car and comes and sits on the grass.

SYLVIE

It's mild today; it's even quite warm for September.

NICOLAS

That's true, Sylvie.

SYLVIE

Life has destroyed me, Nicolas, completely destroyed me. It's horrible, it's so sad; my God, I'm afraid, yes, I'm afraid.

> Nicolas takes off his sports jacket, folds it and puts it on the grass.

NICOLAS

Lie down here if you want.

> Sylvie rests her head on Nicolas' jacket; she sees him now, from her new point of view, in low angle. Nicolas sits on the grass.

SYLVIE

What's your favourite colour?

NICOLAS

I hesitate to answer...I'm trying...

SYLVIE

Mine's scarlet.

NICOLAS

Mine's straw yellow, if I really think about it.

SYLVIE

What time is it?

NICOLAS

Six o'clock. What are you doing tonight?

SYLVIE

I don't know...And I want to do nothing, nothing.

NICOLAS

Absolutely nothing?

SYLVIE

There's one thing I'd like to do, just one: leave right now, cross the border tonight and drive as far as possible...as far as Natchez-under-the-Hill, at the end of Interstate 20.

NICOLAS

Why Natchez-under-the-Hill out of so many American cities? Why that one in particular?

SYLVIE

Why leave tonight? Why drive at night? Why travel so far to get to that particular city, Natchez-under-the-Hill?

NICOLAS

Don't raise your voice, Sylvie. Don't start talking to me like an enemy all of a sudden.

SYLVIE

You shouldn't have switched radio stations a while ago. I was starting to calm down; I was hoping...Then with one flick of your hand you knocked me over. Everything's shattered inside me. All the little pieces of my body are coming apart. It's terrifying, you know. I could feel my belly splitting inside me...and inside my skull I was watching myself dissolve.

> Sylvie speaks calmly, as though the incident in the car had drained her of all energy and separated her from the course of time within her and around her.

SYLVIE

You don't have to make long speeches to me about Natchez-under-the-Hill, Nicolas. I know very well that we won't be crossing the border tonight!

Nicolas takes Sylvie's hand, without saying a word.

SYLVIE

I'm not like the image of me that you've built up. You must be appalled at what happened just now and at how little you know about me. I'm not appalled at anything; I think I can even recognize myself in everything I do. But because you love me, Nicolas...you're unfair, because you want me to be like the woman of your life. Seen from that angle there's something sinister about love, something heartbreaking. The more one loves the more unfair one becomes – what a strange law!

Long shot of the couple lying on the grass (the shot is taken from the north): we can make out the boats anchored in the harbour and, in the late afternoon light, the downtown buildings as straight as columns of figures: so many surfaces and modules without surprise, but not without beauty.

NICOLAS

Why Natchez-under-the-Hill?

SYLVIE

The city is in ruins.

Cut.

Closeup of Sylvie staring at something, her gaze fixed, features petrified. Something crashes near her; she doesn't turn a hair.

NICOLAS

Don't worry about those bumps – the boat has a reinforced hull.

The couple is on the deck of the *Nordnorge*, looking out on a sea afloat with drifting ice. On the horizon we see only glacier particles spread out according to the currents. The boat is halfway between Bjørnøya and the southern tip of Vestspitsbergen. The Barents Sea resembles a field of cotton whose blossoms have begun to open everywhere at the same time, in the space of a few sea miles. This flowering is a counter-metaphor, for the flowers with calices are blocks of ice, powder blue in colour. The waves are neither powerful nor threatening. No gust of wind is raising the Barents Sea as Sylvie and Nicolas scan it from the deck of the Norwegian coastal express-boat: it is as flat as the steppes, long, infinite as a liquid plain, but never silent; for when we are not hearing the rumbling of the friable ice under the hull we hear the melodic tinkling of pieces of ice as they strike against one another during the crossing, we hear the uninterrupted build-up of these frictions, tappings, grindings, bursts of indigo stones which in a few days will turn to liquid in a slate-blue sea. Day and night, the sea gets in tune as though to tackle the first measures of a symphony whose unpredictable score makes its execution forever impossible. No one can escape hearing this unformed melody, which contains all melodies. In the depths of sleep the glacial chorale can still be heard, but it tells nothing: the music of the Barents Sea is light. The notes glide, partly concealed from view, in search of the striking of a mysterious keyboard, which is tuned to the sky. Through this musical induction the atmosphere is impregnated with great softness. The constant sound of the ice creates a fluid and enveloping sound track, all the more fascinating because it is made up not only of *glissandi* but of a cantata without range, without register, which does not stop.

(The last passage, inserted into the screenplay, had no *raison d'être* except to serve as a springboard for the shooting script. This is one of the rare moments in the development of the screenplay when the difficulty of rendering the projected images predisposes one to use a literary kind of descriptive imagery. This is not an admission of filmic impotence, simply an indirect way of writing the screenplay while waiting for this indirect way to be abolished by the supremacy of the images produced. The screenplay is not the film; the breakdown is only one part of the making of the film. It is natural, then, to use shortcuts. In the cinema the reality of descriptions follows their script; in literature the script is the ultimate reality.)

Sylvie is pacing the upper deck of the boat. With her ivy-red sweater she is wearing matching gloves and cap. The wind is rising in the east, the waves are progressively higher, the chunks of powder-blue ice crash into one another more violently. The oceanic symphony is changing register: everything is unfolding in a major key. Terrified by the unleashed sea, Sylvie heads for the cabin.

Direct cut to the inside of the cabin. The curtains are partly open. Nicolas is asleep, fully dressed. Sylvie takes off her sweater and boots. Nicolas does not wake up, even though the boat keeps giving off the sounds of underwater explosions and the wind is blowing stridently through all the chinks in the cabin. Sylvie, wearing her brassiere and underpants, staggers across the rug to close the curtains and give an extra turn of the screw to everything in the cabin that can be closed. The lighting becomes a little darker. Sylvie undresses Nicolas; but he wakes up abruptly, deafened by an apocalyptic din. He stands up on the bed, then realizes that he must sit down. He continues to take off his clothes himself.

Dissolve: Nicolas and Sylvie are lying on the bed in their underclothes, close to each other. A detonation under the side of the ship breaks the *Nordnorge*'s even rolling.

NICOLAS

It's like being on the Titanic.

SYLVIE

The wind's up; you can't imagine how high the waves are.

NICOLAS

Have you still got your sea legs?

SYLVIE

Yes, as long as I'm lying down.

They caress each other a little, kiss with a patience that looks for all the world like a marvellous impatience. The singing softness of the Barents Sea has been metamorphosed into a sustained din that makes everything in the *Nordnorge* vibrate.

The next shots are all exteriors, outside the cabin. Jerky travelling shot on the upper foredeck. High-angle shots to various places on the lower decks where the waves are breaking. Zoom in on the chunks of ice crashing together near the ship. The storm light turns a riot of blue into royal blue. Long shot of two blocks of ice sent crashing into each other by the wind; a multitude of dark blue flashes bursting out in every direction. Take the same shot again immediately, multiply in the extreme the fractions of seconds that precede the contact. When the crash is about to occur again cut to a shot inside cabin 9. Flash of Sylvie and Nicolas. Cut and continue with the crashing of the blocks of ice: the two bodies strike each other, then move apart in slow motion. Cut to the cabin: the flash has occurred, the lovers are pulverized into an infinite number of small phosphorescent cells. A muffled impact is heard under the hull. Nicolas tumbles out of bed, propelled by the forced oscillations of the ship. Nicolas and Sylvie burst out laughing.

Very short sequence. Closeup of Nicolas looking into a mirror. He asks, projecting his voice:

NICOLAS

How do you say *muscles de chagrin* in Norwegian?

Silence. Nicolas moves his eyebrows with his fingers. Freeze frame. Cut.

Nicolas enters the lounge of the *Nordnorge*, joining several passengers and some officers. Nicolas spots the one who he knows speaks French.

NICOLAS

Officer, I didn't understand the message that was just broadcast over the loudspeakers.

OFFICER

Come onto the upper deck with me, Monsieur Vanesse. We can see the southern tip of Spitsbergen through the telescope. It's very powerful.

Nicolas follows him into the wheel-house. The officer adjusts the focus and direction of the telescope. Nicolas looks through the eyepiece.

NICOLAS

I see something white, like an enormous mountain in the middle of the sea. It looks as though there's no storm out there.

OFFICER

Quite right. You can make out the sunny shores. But we still have another two or three hours before we reach the west coast of Spitsbergen. At this latitude the ship has to reduce its speed so it can manoeuvre through the ice more easily.

NICOLAS

Thank you, Officer.

OFFICER

At your service.

Cut.

Cabin number 9. Sylvie has just put on her ski-pants

and hooded raincoat. Nicolas comes back, all out of breath.

NICOLAS

I spotted Svalbard through the captain's telescope. In two or three hours we'll be sailing along the coast of Spitsbergen.

SYLVIE

Fantastic! You know, Nic, I'm ravenous.

NICOLAS

So am I. Let's go have a smørbrød, OK?

Dissolve: Sylvie and Nicolas are sitting at a table near the large bay window in the dining room. She is facing the step, looking down on the Barents Sea which carries an enchanting quantity of glacial memories. The smørbrød platter almost covers the table. Nicolas and Sylvie share a bottle of Italian wine.

SYLVIE

I didn't know the trip was so long and so extraordinary.

NICOLAS

Yes, it's extraordinary.

SYLVIE

I can't tell you how much I'm looking forward to seeing the Svalbard archipelago.

NICOLAS

We won't see the whole archipelago, you know, just two or three islands, mainly Spitsbergen, the biggest one and apparently the most beautiful. The eastern part of the archipelago is uninhabited, I think, and very hard to get to.

SYLVIE

Where did you get the idea of taking us so far away for our honeymoon?

NICOLAS

It had to be something extraordinary, like the end of the world...Very far from everything, and wild.

The sea is calmer now. The ship has stopped turning over with each wave as it did during the storm. Sylvie and Nicolas look out the bay window at the black and white mass of Spitsbergen, which is drawing closer; but it is the *Nordnorge* which is approaching Spitsbergen, not the reverse. They finish eating while the ship advances smoothly heading north.

(A certain solemnity should suffuse this approach to Spitsbergen by boat. The images have no second meaning, but they are the images of a drifting nuptial ceremony. What they contain – floating ice, storm, sea music, wedding night without blackness, unquenchable sun, slow race towards the absolute – are so many elements in the phases of the nuptial rite. The couple, isolated but overseen, is like the *Nordnorge*: partly immersed in the Barents Sea and through it communicating with all seas, all rivers, all tributaries of rivers and all inland seas, as far as Montreal and Sault Sainte-Marie and, through the Mississippi, right to Natchez-under-the-Hill, near Memphis. Their voyage is slow, and more than a voyage – it is an exalted exploration towards the North Pole; they will not arrive there, they will stop just before it, near the great ice-floe which floats like a barrier around the absolute and cannot be crossed. To help the images carry this mass of symbols and tensions, closeups of Sylvie and Nicolas must be added at the approach to Spitsbergen, as though they were standing before the altar in a church with no pilasters, stained-glass windows, double transept, columns, ring-shaped vault, without window tracery or arcature – but not without a nave; and they must say, *mezza voce*, fragments of the sacramental words of the marriage ceremony. Very little and nothing else is enough to confer a planetary extension on the images of the voyage through the Barents Sea. The field of meaning always goes beyond that of reality; even if one wants the latter to equal the former and to conceal it, it never happens. This representation of the nuptial voyage through the Barents Sea, marked by a Phosphorist style, has all the formal peculiarities of the marriage of a man and woman and of their union with all the love on earth.)

> Low-angle shot: Sylvie and Nicolas going down the stairs which join the upper deck to the others. Sylvie is holding Nicolas' arm.

> The Barents Sea is calm now; only the tinkling of masses of ice recalls its presence. Reverse shot: the Spitsbergen coast, very near. Enormous glaciers descend into the sea. Farther away, in perspective, rocky peaks emerge from a dense layer of snow. Some of the summits are very high, but what is particularly striking is their vast number and the grandiose solitude of this cordillera. The pieces of ice beside the ship are of gigantic proportions now, formidable icebergs, floating fortresses which the *Nordnorge* must avoid by slow, precise convolutions. Nicolas and Sylvie hold each other on the deck, staring out at the reflections of the firns and glacial tongues, their attention mobilized by these first images of the Svalbard archipelago. Spitsbergen rises above the sea like the ghost of some cold continent; it is a jungle of glaciers and granitic ridges.

(The landscape inspires as much terror as astonishment; for this reason there is something sacred about the wedding trip to Svalbard. When the great island of Spitsbergen approaches and the *Nordnorge* must take into account, as it proceeds, the ring of icebergs brushing against it, a different rhythm in the flow of sequences is established. For Sylvie and Nicolas the slowness is irresistible. Time continued transcends the components – always decomposable – of temporal discontinuity. The Barents Sea, doubly epicontinental because it borders on a continent and seems to have engendered another, is shot through with small fragments of ice, blue shells, horny tongues – like so many slowly melting discontinuities that will be reborn into the continuity of the seas at the end of their dissolution. The present commentary would be superfluous if it did not contain, in operational reduction, the operational principle of the shooting of the scenes from Tromsø to the southern cape of Spitsbergen. The voyage towards a Pole that, deliberately, will stop short of it, is conceived of as an ascent of the inaccessible. It is not the quest for the absolute which expresses the wedding trip, but the reverse. We set out on an amorous adventure in search of a pre-incorporated absolute. The life that will follow will be only a cone inverted over this short period after the united couple has freely celebrated its own spontaneous joy, to the extent that they will have measured it.)

The west coast of Spitsbergen is gradually revealed as the *Nordnorge* moves north. The clusters of ridges give way to giant coastal cliffs, snowy summits, dark saddles; closeups of Sylvie and Nicolas correspond to this succession. Cut.

Closeup of Nicolas facing a mirror. He asks someone who is probably rather far away from him:

NICOLAS

How do you say *chagrin* in Norwegian?

Silence. Hold the shot longer than its earlier counterpart. Zoom-in on the mirror: Nicolas is looking closely at himself. There are dark circles under his eyes. Then he puts his fingers on his eyebrows. Cut.

Closeup of Sylvie: she is looking away from Spitsbergen, while the escarpments of the cliffs file past in her hair.

SYLVIE

Don't you feel nostalgic about Fortinbras?

NICOLAS

Why nostalgic?

SYLVIE

Because Fortinbras was your last role.

NICOLAS

I think about it sometimes; on the other hand, I'm obsessed by something that has nothing to do with Fortinbras, I mean my own screenplay.

SYLVIE

It's a little crazy to have come this far for our honeymoon.

NICOLAS

Look Sylvie, look!

Sylvie turns to see an enormous lingual block drop into the sea, its fall setting off a tremendous explosion of liquid and sound. The iceberg, still partly on the surface, seems to be struggling so as not to capsize; then it is stabilized and, like the ship, heads northwest, along with all the drifting pieces of ice moving up the west coast of Spitsbergen towards Greenland.

(It goes without saying that the shooting will not necessarily include the same spectacular risks foreseen in the screenplay. Therefore, establish a table of equivalents. For example, it would be easy to replace the breaking away of the tip of a glacier by an avalanche, especially because in a normal summer on Spitsbergen there are a great number of them every day. The same for the storm in the Barents Sea: it is not essential. However, one seldom crosses the Barentshavet without encountering one of these impulsive storms. A contingency margin should be allowed for the production of the film, of any film, in fact; this margin is reduced to the typographic margin in a novel, which writers have been leaving now for centuries. Any representation of the unrepresentable is necessarily subject to dramatic theatrical improvisations.)

SYLVIE

I've had it; I'm going to rest for a while, Nic.

NICOLAS

The boat arrives at Cape Linnaeus in an hour; do you want me to wake you up then?

SYLVIE

No, don't bother.

> Sylvie returns to the cabin. Nicolas stays on deck by himself. A Norwegian passenger offers him his binoculars, with no dialogue. Nicolas accepts the unknown man's offer with many smiles. He adjusts the lenses, sets the focus and looks diligently. Direct cut. Reframe shot with a bicylindrical mask: we see Linda Noble tied up and lying on her back. She moves convulsively, in vexation or rage. Nicolas removes the glasses for an instant, then puts them back to his eyes. Very tight closeup of the ice, swish pans, finally focus on the indentation in the coastline. Jump cut to a long shot of Cape Linnaeus which seems to be moving through the water like a tank. We can distinguish, under the cliff, a minuscule agglomeration towards which the ship is heading. The sea is calm, reflecting the uninterrupted light that warms the snow at the Arctic Circle in summer. It is even warmer at Svalbard because of the Gulf Stream, which makes the west coast of Spitsbergen inhabitable. Nic returns the binoculars to his travelling companion.

> Dissolve: Nicolas sleeping in the cabin while Sylvie looks at the maps on the walls. The boat whistle sounds twice before it moves away from the dock at Cape Linnaeus. A few people watch it go.

SYLVIE

Did you hear the whistle?

NICOLAS

Did I! It woke me up! Was I asleep very long?

SYLVIE

I don't know. I just woke up a few minutes ago myself.

NICOLAS

Where are you going?

SYLVIE

Out on deck. I want to see Cape Linnaeus. Coming?

NICOLAS

Not right now. Fifteen minutes or so...

Sylvie leaves the cabin. Closeup of Nicolas. He is lying on his back, staring at the ceiling. Eva Vos appears, superimposed on his eyes, walking briskly along Lille Grensen. As she approaches the camera stroboscopic pulsations make the image throb, distort it, give it an obsessive cadence. Sound: Nicolas' deeper breathing. The optical pulsations have the effect of making Eva Vos move away from the camera, then approach it, spasmodically. Suddenly her image disappears, giving way to Nicolas' face, from which she has emanated. He gets up, goes into the bathroom, has a close look at his face, decides to shave.

Sylvie, leaning on the foredeck, looking out at the Gulf of Isfjorden which the *Nordnorge* has entered. On both sides of the ship, morainic slags spread out beside the rocky breakwaters, while chunks of ice are obstacles on the surface of the water. After a few bumps and some careful manoeuvring the ship makes its way and goes deeper and deeper into this false-bottomed impasse. The final obstruction is carried away, still further, surprisingly; the depth of the fjord is revealed as the boat enters it, rather as though it were the boat which has engendered the fjord. Isfjorden means Fjord of Ice. In fact, chunks of ice are drifting along the sides of the boat like mystical fish. At the end of a broad bay the Longyearbyen Station appears, with its large buildings.

Dissolve: Sylvie and Nicolas looking at the Longyearbyen Station. The *Nordnorge* edges towards the north-east and sinks deeper still into the belly of Spitsbergen.

SYLVIE

Have a good sleep?

NICOLAS

Yes; I must have been exhausted.

SYLVIE

Did you look out there? It looks like green valleys. Am I dreaming?

NICOLAS

You're right. It's absolutely unbelievable.

Pan towards the east: valleys covered with saxifrage, hills where a timid vegetation grows. The ship enters another narrows: the Billefjorden. It's as though one were in a new country, almost human, almost temperate. It's late by continental time, but so what! For the night is as indiscernible as the day. The sun, sister of the moon, is shining brightly over the Billefjorden. An unreal country comes bursting out from the four points of the compass as the fjord narrows and the slopes of ice and snow come closer to the sides of the ship. This is not a miracle, but there is something miraculous about it all the same: in the deepest part of the fjord, where there is nothing to hint at this discovery, it is as though one were in a desert with white and blue pyramids looming out of it. The first sight is striking: it is not Egypt or the desert, but just as blinding, and the pyramids really are pyramids. The Billefjorden is only a cove of the Isfjorden, but it is also a magic, blissful valley, a white combe strewn with pyramids.

Objective ellipse: the *Nordnorge* does not put into port at Pyramiden (at least not in the film), so after this entry into the Billefjorden it makes a half-turn. What has been seen on the way there is presented again, but in the opposite direction. Landscapes already seen are now unrecognizable: the light of the sun has changed by several degrees, the shadows of the treetops have moved as on a sundial. Pyramiden has not been seen or even glimpsed, it is only hinted at, at the end of a too perfect valley. It is the Djebel Amour, unknown and unknowable.

Dissolve: the ship emerging from the Isfjorden, hugging its northern bank. The *Nordnorge* heads towards the Pole again, hugging the west coast of Spitsbergen even closer. To the west, the horizon is obstructed by Prince Charles Island, a long island without relief where there is a natural harbour. Nicolas and Sylvie are leaning on the rail, scrutinizing the coast, where there is more and more contrast. This is, in fact, an impression based on the cumulative effect of the voyage. Landscapes seen earlier are added up for the viewer, as they are for Sylvie and Nicolas. A gradation is established.

Direct cut: Eva Vos sitting at a table on the terrace of the Studenterlunden café in Oslo. Subjective camera. The person Eva is speaking to is looking at her. She smiles, adjusts a lock of hair, gives the person a long, even provocative look. Beginning with this shot, optical pulsations begin to dilate and contract the image, following a cadence twice the speed of the rhythm of the heart. Eva Vos' face comes closer, moves away, is drawn out, concentrated. She smiles and says to her interlocutor:

EVA VOS
And do I have muscles of chagrin?

Eva Vos, bantering, keeps coming closer to the lens; the image moves off centre and pivots outside its axis. Cut.

Dining room of the *Nordnorge*.

SYLVIE
Will there be a part for me in your film?

NICOLAS
Maybe.

SYLVIE

What kind of character?

NICOLAS

A woman, twenty-two, blonde, married for a few days.

SYLVIE

What kind of personality?

NICOLAS

Yours.

SYLVIE

You're teasing me.

NICOLAS

No, I'm not.

SYLVIE

I wonder if I'd like to play myself.


(There's no need to be familiar with the Arabic theory of trepidation to know that the *Nordnorge* is in sight of Ny Ålesund, that it has only a few more lengths to go before arriving in port.)


The water in the Kongsfjorden is as smooth as the surface of a mirror. The mountains are in an unstable equilibrium with the water. The *Nordnorge* is troubling the Lakist gentleness which impregnates this flowerless, treeless landscape. Sylvie and Nicolas look silently at the sumptuous, peaceful bay. The tinkling sound of floating ice reverberates at the end of the fjord and is amplified by its own echo. The harbour. The mooring mast at Ny Ålesund. The boat has arrived in port.

An impressive welcome for an out-of-the-way station. Most of the passengers are met with great pomp and invited to get into the snow-launch that will take them to their destination. The Arctic Hotel's snow-launch is near the wharf. Sylvie and Nicolas are swallowed up in it along with other passengers from the *Nordnorge*. It is very warm inside. The driver gets into the large vehicle last. It goes in a semi-circle, then up a gentle slope.

Ny Ålesund: a group of rather undifferentiated buildings, various styles of apartment blocks, a few private houses. The Arctic Hotel is a fairly modern three-storey building.

Dissolve: while Sylvie finishes putting away the contents of their suitcases Nicolas looks out the window at the other shore of the Kongsfjorden, at the incredible Kongsbreen glacier which from this vantage point swallows up the entire landscape and quenches its thirst, one might suppose, in the waters of the fjord, through its numerous tentacles of ice. There is something fantastic and horrifying about this glacier, a white octopus. Nicolas can't help feeling a certain anguish. He turns towards the inside of the room: there are prints of the Hornsundtind, of Jan Mayen Island and Ny Ålesund on the walls.

NICOLAS

Know what I'd like to do? Take a rest from the sea for a few hours. It's painful, never being able to escape from all this light.

SYLVIE

You aren't getting sleepy by any chance?

NICOLAS

No, absolutely not.

SYLVIE

Let's go shopping. There must be a store in Ny Ålesund.

NICOLAS

All right. And I can stock up on Aquavit.

Cut.

(The perception of time is undoubtedly linked to the technical means man uses to gain time or to kill it. In the days of Apianus' quadrant, time fled irretrievably, according to Horatian predictability. The invention of the wheel modified this representation: time that can be compressed can also be decompressed, although it is subject to an insurmountable determinism. This is no longer the case. In this film, the perception of time responds to a printed circuit system. The tempo of the story results from a series of selective operations. By pushing a button we inform time of its instantaneous filmic framework: the flashback is inextricably mixed with what is to come, the anticipatory flash is organized according to the same self-regulating intrusive system, the order of the sequences is defined as a deliberate dislocation of the relationship between the viewer's time and the time of the plot. The perception of time is modelled on its mental image; besides, temporal reproduction invariably overflows the field of the present. The present resembles a palatine membrane between what has just ended and what has not yet begun. Time perceived is necessarily in the past, which is a way of saying that the present has an aftertaste of memory and the projected future is only a future memory, thus a past to come! This notional tangle is a tangle only in appearance; it is the same for the film. If we do not recognize ourselves in it immediately, we know very well that it will come, because the future of the plot will provide only a past which had not yet been revealed when the viewer was concerned about it. Ever since Sylvie and Nicolas crossed the Arctic Circle their days have been destructured by losing their caesurae. The slowness or speed of the film is not objective data but subjective connotations that correspond to the viewer's serenity or anguish. The *tempus continuatum* transmutes transitive time into an immanent time and it is hard for the viewer to imagine how he will be able to get out of it. The film unwinds in a completely random manner: the system is unpredictable and it would be futile to try to predict it because any attempt at prediction would imply that the subsequent phases of the film are not a past that is yet to come. Thus the unpredictable is linked to the structure of the printed circuit (for as we advance we do not know in what manner it will be printed) and not to factual suspense. The formant form of the film rebounds through its own dispositions, not through the exterior unwinding that it represents.)

Dining room of the Arctic Hotel at Ny Ålesund. Nicolas and Sylvie appear at the entry. The maître d'hôtel shows them to a table close to a grill capped with a chimney shaped like an inverted funnel. The restaurant is filled to capacity. Civil servants, likely, mining engineers, the town's leading citizens and two travellers eating a meal in the only hostelry on the Svalbard archipelago.

SYLVIE

I'm hungry.

Two waitresses wearing Norwegian blue dresses, pleated in the old style but with hems that stop at mid-thigh, keep crossing the dining room of the Arctic Hotel. In the centre stands the master of the show, the chef who prepares the grilled meats, seasons and flames them. Sylvie is absorbed in reading the menu and Nicolas is watching the feverish activity in the grill room.

Swish pan to the right: Sylvie, in a dress the colour of gypsum flowers, is standing with a glass in her hand, speaking to two or three people who form a circle around her. Context of worldly ceremony: everyone is dressed up. Sylvie is radiant; her hair is curled, cut short at the nape of her neck, and her eyes, faintly lined with blue, stand out against her pale skin. Zoom in on her: she turns towards the camera (subjective for this shot) and smiles; but there is something fixed about her smile because immediately Sylvie, isolated by the centring and more particularly by the metamorphosis which occurs in her and which she cannot hide, moves slowly towards the very centre of the lens which seems to perforate her between the breasts, at the bottom of her décolletage. Quick reverse shot: Nicolas, in a dark suit with a vest and pocket handkerchief, walking towards Sylvie. Long shot: we can glimpse a buffet table, a large number of guests. At the back of the room Sylvie and Nicolas approach each other, kiss on both cheeks. They look at each other, fascinated, as though they were alone on a floating island, separated from the others by a system of ponds, straits and canals. High-angle medium shot to Sylvie.

SYLVIE

I didn't expect to see you here.

NICOLAS

The producer's a friend of mine. But what about you? What are you doing here? Are you still at Vincent d'Indy?

SYLVIE

What am I doing here...?

NICOLAS

Never mind, don't answer.

SYLVIE

How long has it been?

NICOLAS

A month, I think.

SYLVIE

A month's a long time. You know, it's very upsetting to see you again.

NICOLAS

Why?

SYLVIE

Because...because this time I haven't forgotten your name, Nicolas Vanesse!

NICOLAS

Would you like to have supper Chez Bardet after the screening?

SYLVIE

I can't, I'm with somebody.

NICOLAS

Well, in that case...

> He walks away from Sylvie, who is very disconcerted to see him break off their meeting. Nicolas takes two or three steps, then comes back to Sylvie.

NICOLAS

There's something I have to tell you. You're beautiful, absolutely marvellous, but I can't remember your name...

SYLVIE

Sylvie Dubuque.

> Closeup of Sylvie in the dining room of the Arctic Hotel at Ny Ålesund. Nicolas looks distracted.

SYLVIE

I'll start with the *oeufs Meurette*...what about you?

NICOLAS

Smørbrød for the first course.

> The waitress notes their orders and waits patiently for the rest.

NICOLAS

I'm in the mood for a Châteaubriand.

SYLVIE

Me too!

NICOLAS

A bottle of Château Lebrock, please.

> The waitress walks away from the newlyweds' table.

SYLVIE

Ny Ålesund is fantastic!

NICOLAS

I didn't expect to find a gourmet restaurant so close to the North Pole.

There is a festive atmosphere in the restaurant where Roald Amundsen had a snack before his flight to the North Pole and where Nobile ate his last meal. Huge photographs set into the walls show the *Fram* stuck in the great ice pack, explorers, the dirigible *Italia* rising above the Kongsfjorden before a crowd of spectators on the wharf at Ny Ålesund.

The waitress brings the *oeufs Meurette* and the smør-brød. Immediately, the maître d'hôtel brings the Château Lebrock, shows the label and uncorks the bottle. Nicolas is delighted with the wine, and the maître d'hôtel pours some into their glasses. Sylvie takes a sip. Freeze frame when she raises her chin.

Closeup of Nicolas frowning as he watches Sylvie. A fit of absent-mindedness paralyses him and gives him a mask of absence.

Shot inside the Ford Torino parked in an alley alongside Parc Lafontaine: this time the image allows us to iden-tify Sylvie visually. She throws herself wildly onto Nicolas, who submits willingly; his initial passivity changes to a kind of unbridled immobility. Nicolas shouts out his pleasure as Sylvie bends over him, but she immediately removes herself from him and spits what was in her mouth onto the floor of the car.

SYLVIE

You know, I don't remember your name...

The evocation continues in two ways: visually, the scene in the car begins again eight times in succession, the last image in the sequence linked with the first as in

a loop and then the accompanying sound-track is as follows:

NICOLAS

Hello, Sylvie Dubuque.

SYLVIE

I prefer just plain Sylvie. Is that all right with you?

NICOLAS

This is the third time we've met.

SYLVIE

But why should we see each other again? You'll never forget
how we met and what I did... You'll never forget it, I'm sure of
that, unfortunately!

NICOLAS

You weren't really yourself; let's not talk about it any more.
When I saw you again at the Film Board the other night I
thought you were very beautiful...I recognized you by your
eyes, I think. Your eyes reassure me. There's something very
gentle in you, something very precious...

SYLVIE

Nicolas, it's hard for me to believe what you're telling me.

NICOLAS

You've got no choice.

SYLVIE

Maybe I'll believe you if you tell me often enough...

The scene in the Ford Torino is interrupted, the last
time, just after Sylvie has spat out Nicolas' sperm. Cut.

Dining room in the Arctic Hotel at Ny Ålesund. Closeup of Nicolas, staring, his features frozen. Reverse shot:
Sylvie sipping her wine.

SYLVIE

I've never tasted such a splendid wine. Will you buy us some
when we get back to Montreal, Nic?

The waitress arrives with two grilled Châteaubriands, arranged on large plates with *pommes gaufrées* and braised endive. Nicolas takes advantage of her arrival to order another bottle of Château Lebrock.

SYLVIE

That's too much, Nicolas.

NICOLAS

Come on, drink it up. Besides, what I'd really like to do is order another Châteaubriand, this one's so good.

SYLVIE

You'd think you were leaving for the North Pole after supper.

NICOLAS

With a little luck they might have some cheese.

The waitress comes with the bottle of wine, tells him there is no cheese, but there is an excellent pâté of ptarmigan, a house specialty. Nicolas agrees to order some.

SYLVIE

I've never seen you enjoy your food so much.

Dissolve: Nicolas attacks the ptarmigan pâté and pours himself a generous amount of wine. Sylvie looks dreamily at the posters of Amundsen and the still sun-lit landscape of the Kongsfjorden which we catch a glimpse of through the large panes of glass. The sun seems to defy everything, even the daily passage into night; suddenly a poignant strangeness seeps into the life of Ny Ålesund. The light that one can never flee, anywhere, at any time, except by closing one's eyes, is somehow intolerable.

Dissolve: the camera is on the wharf at Ny Ålesund. Four passengers are boarding the Arctic Hotel's cabin cruiser. We recognize Sylvie and Nicolas, both warmly dressed and carrying back packs. The cabin cruiser starts up rapidly (keep the same frame and follow it) and moves away from the wharf, heading towards the mouth of the Kongsfjorden. For this series of sequences, the camera is on board the Arctic Hotel's boat. The passengers are all absorbed in contemplating Cape Mitra, which rises up at the western entrance to the fjord like a sentinel: its furrowed mask is reminiscent of an enormous, cracked high-relief. The cabin cruiser forges ahead into the Arctic Ocean at high speed: its weight and construction allow it to manoeuvre quickly, and its hull has a steel wale around it enabling it to run into the small ice splinters which loom up unexpectedly on the waves with no danger. The cruise to the north of Cape Mitra proceeds at a staggering speed that contrasts with the ponderous advance of the *Nordnorge*. The summits of Spitsbergen have nothing in common now with human landscapes: they are dry crests, black rakes, rocky bars, horns of Cernunnos, toothed crests. The Spitsbergen seems like the product of a Dantesque delirium. During this portion of the trip the images must force the note of strangeness and discomfort; nothing must attenuate the monstrous aspect and the plateresque style of these superfluous pieces of ice and this unreal island.

(The unbiased viewer is wondering whether Spitsbergen really exists, whether these mountainous asperities are part of a very successful maquette. If he doubts the real existence of Spitsbergen he is probably repressing his feelings before what he believes to be an orgy of trickery or some geographic imposture. Of course, a person on guard can also find a way to question the validity of his scepticism. It is possible, too, that memories of what he has read will remind the viewer, already shaken, that the existence of Svalbard is known only through a reference in the Landnamabok, which dates from the thirteenth century, when Thule, the Greenland ice cap and even *Nova Zembla*, the archipelago in the Arctic Ocean that Gottfried Wilhelm Leibniz found so fascinating, were already known. The viewer wonders too why the honey-moon of Sylvie and Nicolas Vanesse is unfolding in this context, which is as unlikely as it is artificial; this last route moves imperceptibly away from the first and, following a decentring inscribed in the scenario, makes the viewer want to understand the nuptial system of symbols rather than satisfy his curiosity about the geography.)

After the Chain of the Seven Glaciers, the Magdalene-fjorden opens up, cuts into the western flank of Spits-bergen at the far north of the large island. The pieces of ice seem to conspire against any traffic inside the bay, but the boat, well protected, makes its way to the end of the fjord. It accosts a rocky breakwater that leads to a pebble beach strewn with black rocks.

NICOLAS

OK. Forty-eight hours from now.

Nicolas and Sylvie say goodbye to the other passengers and the pilot. The boat heads north, as far as the large ice-pack. Sylvie and Nicolas watch it move away across water mined with chunks of ice; collisions cause it to deviate from its course and force the pilot to perform certain manoeuvres to set the boat right.

NICOLAS

Notice how mild it is?

SYLVIE

Yes; I don't think I need my windbreaker here.

They move along the docking area, cross an area appallingly congested with black blocks. Sylvie slips on an icy incline and lies lazily on the ground. Closeup of Sylvie: she is looking at something very close to her. Choppy series of shots showing human burials, piled up haphazardly. Black wooden chests are ripped open. Sylvie gets up, terrified.

SYLVIE

Nicolas!!!!

NICOLAS

Did you hurt yourself?

SYLVIE

Look: here, there, all around...they're human skeletons!

Nicolas retraces his steps, holds his hand out to Sylvie and climbs with her over what does, in fact, look like an ancient human cemetery. The evidence is blinding: it is indeed a glacial cemetery, a disturbing reminder of the occupation of Spitsbergen by Dutch whalers in the sixteenth century. Nicolas picks up a skull.

NICOLAS

How long will a man lie i' th' earth ere he rot?...That skull had a tongue in it, and could sing once! Here's a skull now hath lien you i' th' earth three-and-twenty years...Here hung those lips that I have kissed I know not how oft...

SYLVIE

Stop it, Nicolas, you're making me sick. You can't imagine what it felt like, lying next to those skeletons...

NICOLAS

I was just quoting a few lines from Shakespeare...Don't get so upset.

Nicolas throws the skull towards the fjord with all his might; it smashes to bits against a rock.

SYLVIE

Nicolas, let's get out of here.

The newlyweds go towards the foothills of the mountains. Walking along this riverside plateau is easy.

Dissolve: the couple is walking along a gently sloping winding mountain path; they come to a level stretch dominated by a diminutive overhang. In two tries, and without using their rope, Sylvie and Nicolas hoist themselves up onto the overhang which looks out, not on the fjord and its cemetery that has been profaned by erosion, but onto a gulf at the end of which, on the other side, is an enormous thalweg. At the bottom of the hill we can distinguish a groove, which spreads like a cornice up to the summit.

Dissolve: Nicolas breaking the path. Spots of sulphur-coloured moss appear at the base of the rocks most exposed to the light, a few cloudberries too, and some glistening scabious.

Series of dissolves from various points along the way: Nicolas and Sylvie finally come to a shelf where the cornice begins, from three to six feet wide, suspended from a thalweg. The path is covered here and there with hardened, very slippery snow, and sometimes strewn with ice and rocky debris.

Dissolve: shots taken from a lookout at the peak of the Haraldkrone. From this point we have a bird's-eye view onto Magdalena Bay. Multiple shots during this dialogue.

SYLVIE

I've been shaking ever since I saw the cemetery and even though the scenery is lovely I've still got a lump in my throat.

NICOLAS

If you don't let yourself go, your fear is going to contaminate any impressions you might get of Spitsbergen. According to the map there should be a shelter right here, on this plateau. You stay here; I'll go and look.

SYLVIE

No, don't leave me alone. I'll come with you.

Dissolve: Sylvie coming out of the shelter to go and get some fresh snow. Inside the log cabin, Nicolas is unfolding a large map of Spitsbergen. Sylvie comes back with a saucepan filled with snow.

SYLVIE

Come and see how the sky's clouding over!

> Nicolas leaves the shelter with Sylvie. There is a low
> cloud ceiling and the wind is blowing fiercely from the
> northeast. A murmur fills the air: it is the tinkling sound
> of chunks of ice colliding in the bay.

NICOLAS

Here it comes.

> Large flakes of snow suddenly begin to fall.

SYLVIE

Phoo, we're going to have a lot of time to kill. Come on, I'll
make you a nice meal!

> It does not seem like an exceptional precipitation; all of
> Spitsbergen is a wayside shelter of snow and ice that
> one hundred and fifty days of uninterrupted sunlight do
> not manage to melt – or only slightly. Nicolas lights the
> alcohol lamp inside the shelter. The two windows in the
> hut are not enough to light the inside: the opaque snow
> breaks the limpidezza of the heights to which Sylvie
> and Nicolas were growing accustomed. Everything is
> matte; nothing reflects. The landscape is abolished. The
> snow gives way to an image of reality characterized by
> its own colour as much as by the absence of all colour.

> Dissolve: Sylvie lying on the floor in front of the fire she
> has lit, sound asleep. A meticulous peace reigns inside
> the shelter. A kind of sluggishness takes over every-
> thing that is alive and everything that is conscious, and
> is even translated in formal terms by a tendency to-
> wards fixity.

(The metaphoric paralysis which strikes the film does not
spare the viewer. Here the viewer's passivity reaches what
we might call its paroxysm. The snow is falling silently; and
the film, so we might think, suspends reality which, through

a decelerated sidereal orbitation, is plunged into a restorative lethargy. Few films contain moments of respite, dead periods really, and yet in real life we often bless those moments of lassitude which follow periods of movement. A touch of lassitude, nothing more, makes the representation of Sylvie and Nicolas' wedding trip more adequate. It's not so much that the viewer will disconnect, for it is really the film which is disconnected from the viewer. If the viewer becomes aware of this pseudo-defection by the film in time, he will be quick to consider it a dramatic lacuna, not an attempt by the filmmaker to put himself in unison with the viewer, and a concentrated effort at participation at the most passive level: the level of fatigue. This expedition through the heights around the Magdalenefjorden is exhausting; living kills.)

Interior. Shelter. The meal is finished. Sylvie is putting away her cooking utensils, tidying things around the fire. Nicolas stands up, goes to get his bottle of Aquavit, which he had stuck in the snow at the entrance to the shelter.

NICOLAS

Now I won't open the door again. We'll keep the heat inside...

Nicolas drinks some Aquavit from the bottle. Sylvie puts another log on the fire, stirs it up, watches it for a while.

NICOLAS

Do you want a sip?

SYLVIE

Just a bit, it burns.

Sylvie drinks from the bottle too. She hands it back to him.

SYLVIE

I know it's good.

Nicolas is very close to Sylvie who is kneeling in front of the firelace, still tidying up.

NICOLAS

I'm going to take your clothes off.

SYLVIE

Nicolas...

Sylvie puts down what she was holding and before she has time to turn all the way around towards Nicolas he is on top of her. He unbuttons her blouse first, then undoes the snap between the cups of her brassiere.

SYLVIE

Not on the floor...

NICOLAS

Just let yourself go, Sylvie.

SYLVIE

I'm afraid you're going to tear my slacks, love; here, I'll take them off.

NICOLAS

Let me undress you, Sylvie.

Nothing less than frenzy can describe Nicolas' haste. He helps Sylvie take off her nacarat slacks and everything else she is wearing.

SYLVIE

How will we know when it's tomorrow?

Cut.

Establishing shot of the shore of the Magdalenefjorden in the same place where the Arctic Hotel canoe left Sylvie and Nicolas, just beside the sinister whalers' cemetery. Long still shot: in the distance we can see Nicolas running towards the shore, distraught. He stops very close to the camera and sits down on a black block. He is prostrate; he holds his head in his hands. Closeup of his right hand. Dissolve to black.

The boat pilot shakes Nicolas' shoulders and speaks to him in Norwegian. Nicolas seems virtually comatose; he does not emerge from the too deep sleep which has taken hold of him. One of the passengers steps out of the boat onto the shore and joins Nicolas and the pilot.

DOCTOR LARSEN

Come now, sir, what can I do for you?

NICOLAS

We have to go back. We have to go back.

He points his finger vaguely in the direction from which he has come running.

DR. LARSEN

Is your wife hurt?

Nicolas gets his breath back with difficulty while the pilot tells Dr. Larsen who Nicolas is.

DR. LARSEN

Come on, Mr. Vanesse, I'm a doctor...I'm going to take care of Mrs. Vanesse. But you have to tell me where she is. Did she fall?

NICOLAS

Yes, she fell!

DR. LARSEN

What condition is she in? Does she know we're coming? What did you tell her when you left?

NICOLAS

I don't know.

DR. LARSEN

You must tell me, Mr. Vanesse, you must!

NICOLAS

I can't take any more, I can't take any more...

DR. LARSEN

Try to get hold of yourself, Mr. Vanesse. We'll leave right

away and we'll help your wife. Come on, get up. You're going to take us to her.

Nicolas remains prostrate, not saying a single word or making a single gesture. The doctor says a few words in Norwegian to his wife, who is still on the deck of the boat. She leaps to the ground immediately, bringing her husband a leather-covered flask.

DR. LARSEN

Here, Mr. Vanesse, drink this. You need it.

He holds out a little hunter's cup which Nicolas drains in one gulp as he looks Dr. Larsen in the eyes.

NICOLAS

I think she's seriously hurt. She fell to the bottom of a ravine. I heard her shout...

Long silence. The pilot, the doctor and his wife are stupefied.

DR. LARSEN

Were you able to talk to her after she fell?

NICOLAS

No...

DR. LARSEN

How did it happen?

NICOLAS

We were very close to the Dronningmaudbreen, down below there. And we had to rope down before we came to a stopping place...I went ahead as I usually do; besides, we could talk to each other during the ascent...Then she said, "I'm ready..."

Nicolas stops his recitation; once again he buries his head in his hands, silent, collapsed. The pilot exchanges a few words with Dr. Larsen.

DR. LARSEN

Mr. Bukdahl, our pilot, tells me that he knows the massif where you were climbing very well.

NICOLAS

Then he'll show us the way.

> Dr. Larsen and the pilot exchange a few more words in
> Norwegian. A long silence follows. The pilot goes back
> to the canoe.

NICOLAS

We were on our way to the shelter at Skarho...According to
the guidebook we just had an hour's walk, no more...

> Interior. Boat. Bukdahl communicates with Ny Åle-
> sund by radio. From the radio station we can see Nico-
> las, Dr. Larsen and his wife on the other shore. Bukdahl
> ends his conversation, rejoins the group; he and Dr.
> Larsen speak.

> All this time Nicolas looks around with no apparent
> emotion; he expresses nothing and seems almost not in-
> volved. He is elsewhere, in the depths of a solitude
> which walls him in.

DR. LARSEN

Mr. Vanesse, I've got some good news: the Norwegian government helicopter will be here in less than an hour. It's the
only thing to do, with this rigorous climate and the difficulty
of mountain searches. While we're waiting come inside the
cabin and get warm...

> Nicolas lets himself be led on board the boat, its motor
> still running to keep the temperature in the cabin com-
> fortable. Nicolas sits at a table in the lounge with Dr.
> Larsen and his wife while the pilot, standing on the
> foredeck, watches the sky.

DR. LARSEN

Of course it's been snowing almost without let-up for two
days...

NICOLAS

I know, I know.

DR. LARSEN

That doesn't make things any easier.

Dissolve: we hear the sound of a helicopter. Everyone is scrutinizing the cloud ceiling. Sound of a detonation: the pilot has just let off a signal rocket, which leaves an orange trail in the sky before it drops onto the ice of the fjord. The helicopter is in sight; it heads for the beach, very close to the spot where the Arctic boat is tied up. As the helicopter lands it stirs up a cloud of snow, which makes everything disappear instantaneously in a white powder. Then the blades slow down and the helicopter becomes visible again. The helicopter pilot goes inside the cabin cruiser. He unfolds a very detailed map of Spitsbergen on the table; everyone leans over the map.

DR. LARSEN

Mr. Vanesse, you'll have to show us as precisely as you can what path you took.

Nicolas goes over to the table; someone hands him a red felt pen and puts down a transparent sheet so that he can draw lines on it and retrace them, without messing up the map.

Dissolve. Shots on board the Norwegian government helicopter. Dr. Larsen, the boat pilot, the helicopter pilot and Nicolas are in the little machine, which is flying very close to the spurs of the mountains around the Magdalenefjorden. Nicolas indicates the route to take, hesitating at times. The helicopter climbs up the glaciers, hangs suspended above ravines, brushes against the combes.

Dissolve: Nicolas gives directions to the pilot who is manoeuvring his machine along the rocky faces, brings it to a stop at certain places, then resumes the same course again, more slowly. The helicopter plunges into valleys, skims the ground, heaves up towards the sky, starts again. The helicopter starts from the spines at the peaks and through numerous plunges analyzes the configuration of Spitsbergen. The trajectories of the flight are repeated, overlap, are superimposed on one another in a dizzying gyration. Cut.

Nicolas getting out of a taxi. He pays the bill, takes his single suitcase and goes into the Hotel Linnea in Trondheim. Shots in the lobby, then in the reception area.

NICOLAS

Just one night. I'm flying to Oslo tomorrow morning. Here's my ticket. Would you be kind enough to make the reservation with the airline? Thanks very much.

Nicolas walks away from the reception desk. The clerk holds Nicolas' ticket up to his eyes. He dials a number on the telephone. Zoom-in on the writing on the ticket: *Mr. and Mrs. Nicolas Vanesse.* He hesitates, interrupts his call, looks at the registration form Nicolas has just filled in. Another hesitation, then he picks up the telephone.

CLERK

Mr. Vanesse, I apologize for disturbing you. It's about your plane ticket. The reservation's in the names of Mr. and Mrs. Vanesse. Should I confirm two seats on flight 850 for Oslo... Just for you, then.

Shot in Nicolas' room.

NICOLAS

Ask them to make out the other part of the ticket for my wife, but to leave the date open. Thanks.

Nicolas hangs up. He takes a few steps, pensive; he stops at the window which overlooks part of the old city and the second last loop of the Nidelva. In the centre of this urban landscape rises the octagonal mass of the cathedral. Nicolas presses his nose and forehead against the window and looks out. Dissolve: the telephone ringing. Nicolas picks up the receiver. Direct cut to the reception office.

CLERK

Mr. Vanesse, your seat is reserved on flight 850 tomorrow

morning. And in about an hour I'll have your ticket and Madame's. I've sent a messenger to take care of it. Everything will be left in your box.

Nicolas hangs up and collapses onto the bed. Superimposed on the frozen image of his face, the enormous glacial octopus of the Kongsbreen as Nicolas saw it from the room in the Arctic Hotel at Ny Ålesund.

Dissolve: the front lobby of the Hotel Linnea. Nicolas gets out of the elevator, greets the reception clerk who recognizes him.

NICOLAS

It's me again...would you have a telegraph form, please?

The clerk hands him two or three. Nicolas slips them into his wallet and walks towards the door. He is wearing the same sweater he had on when he arrived at the hotel. From the top of the hotel steps Nicolas watches the traffic on Sondregate. Then, hands in his pockets, he sets off along the sidewalk, mingling with the crowd. The streets of the old city are inordinately broad and spacious, conferring an unchangeable splendour on Saint Olav's capital. Nicolas walks to the Fjordgaten where the cool wind announces that summer is over. He walks beside the water, looking helpless; he leans on the parapet, looks out at the fjord for some time, then leaves again, visibly not knowing what to do with his time. He goes back to the heart of old Nidaros, walking along Nordregate. Nicolas lets himself be carried away by Trondheim's liveliness and charm, walking more slowly than the other passers-by, stopping along the way several times, occasionally staring at the other passers-by, who stare back at him. He goes into a café, orders a Bokkøl. He puts the telegraph forms on the table. He fills in the first one. Closeup of what he is writing in block letters: Eva Vos. He stops there; he utters some inaudible words. The moment comes when he must fill in the space for the message: he orders another beer, writes in one burst, several words at once.

NICOLAS
Serious climbing accident at Svalbard. Sylvie disappeared; search continues. Arrive Oslo tomorrow flight 850 from Trondheim.

> Nicolas crumples the form, then tears it up. He starts again on another form.

NICOLAS
Eva Vos, NRK, Oslo. Sylvie fell to her death while climbing. Arrive Oslo tomorrow flight 850 from Trondheim. Nicolas Vanesse.

> Nicolas leaves the telegram where he can see it. He reaches over and picks up the London *Times*, wound around a wooden rod. He looks at the date: July 20, 1973.

(Something's wrong here: time appears to Nicolas in the form of an antedated document. The *Zeitbewusstsein* is out of joint; and yet, time is the best known thing in the world. In theory, everyone is endowed with an awareness of time which surpasses all human faculties in acuteness and adaptability. It's all useless: the *Times* is out of date. Nicolas, who is trying to date Sylvie's death by referring to the English newspaper, is making a fatal mistake in his dating, reducing Sylvie's existential *ablauf* by four or five days. Memories printed on paper do not coincide with Nicolas' reference points. Tomorrow I was, yesterday I shall be. Time carries everything away according to a diagram that is always the same, known by everyone and yet at times difficult to reinvent through memory alone. We do not leaf through time, it is time that plucks the petals off our lives. Nicolas puts back the *Times*. The strangeness of this sequence in Trondheim paradoxically neutralizes its expressionism; through his Caligarian operation time is reduced to the awareness of *contretemps*. Nothing is expressed: the drowned woman has disappeared to the amphidromical point from which everything that flows, flows. Nicolas remembers an illuminated theatre, but this reflexive dimension cannot be translated into images.)

The day topples slowly; the streets of Trondheim are filled with people walking in every direction. Nicolas, looking pensive, follows shadows, contemplates the fragments of sky between the buildings. He does not stop in front of the watchmaker's window, but continues to walk with the same absentminded rhythm along Kjøpmanngate, flanked on both sides by the arrogant façades of Hanseatic privateers. The Nidelva flows just behind, a soluble street in the centre of the port city.

Dissolve: Nicolas going through the front door of the Hotel Linnea again; he walks up to the reception clerk who is holding a large envelope.

CLERK

Your tickets. Everything's arranged for tomorrow morning. The plane leaves at ten to nine.

NICOLAS

Tell me, what date is it today?

CLERK

The twenty-eighth, sir.

NICOLAS

What month.

CLERK

July...The year, perhaps?

NICOLAS

If it isn't too much trouble.

CLERK

1973.

NICOLAS

Thank you, thank you very much.

CLERK

At your service, sir.

Nicolas walks away from the reception desk, takes a few steps in the lobby, returns to the reception clerk, who can't conceal his surprise.

NICOLAS

I forgot this telegram. Here's the message. Do you have the correct time?

CLERK

Six sixteen, Mr. Vanesse.

> Direct cut to the interior of the airplane with Nicolas inside. The Oslo airport at Fornebu spreads out below the fuselage. Nicolas feels a tug at his heart as he looks at this landscape which he and Sylvie discovered together a few days earlier, after crossing the Atlantic. Long shot of the airplane which lands, turns into one of the deferent corridors leading to the airport. The passengers leave the plane. Nicolas gets out, holding his sweater and carrying the small suitcase. He enters the main lobby, looks around, appearing distracted. He sits on a couch placed well within view of the main entrance to the airport.

(Transitive time passes badly. It is a burden that the film must bear by transforming substance into cloud. Yes, transitive time flows according to a braking transience, while the other, the immanent time of joy and love, is defined as the breath of beauty. Nicolas' little suitcase is Sylvie's symbolic coffin. He keeps her body, enclosed in a coffer, close to him; he carries it, but the weight of the body drags him along, determines how he will walk and what his destiny will be. The veil of the unspeakable has just been torn.)

> Nicolas in a telephone booth at Fornebu.

NICOLAS

Eva? Eva Vos? It's Nicolas Vanesse.

> Direct cut to Eva Vos' bedroom. She is dragging herself out of bed, holding the telephone. She sits on the edge of the bed, wearing a very short nightgown.

EVA

No, I didn't get your telegram...I never go to the office over the weekend and this is Sunday. You didn't know it was Sunday? But why are you calling me from Svalbard?

Closeup of Nicolas.

NICOLAS

I've just arrived at the airport...in Oslo. I have to see you today. Don't ask too many questions, I beg you. I'll be at the Fønix in half an hour – I've checked my bags there; I want to meet you in an hour. Tell me the name of a restaurant and I'll be there...Skansen. All right.

Eva's bedroom: she hangs up, bewildered. Her hair is uncombed, there are light blue pouches under her eyes. The camera follows her in medium shot (signifying covetous desire): she opens the shutters, letting a luminous discharge pour into her bedroom. Her arms and face are deeply tanned. She stands at the window for a moment, looking at the wooded hills separating her from Oslo. The day is already hot. Eva Vos walks out of range of the camera when she begins to take off her nightgown. Cut.

The taxi with Nicolas in it is travelling briskly along the grille of the Slottsparken: the city is almost deserted. Nicolas recognizes some familiar landscapes as he passes them; but this city, without cars or almost, without activity, is more like a city of the imagination.

Eva Vos' apartment. She is wearing white slacks and walking around her bedroom bare-breasted. She adjusts her brassiere, puts on her jacket in front of the mirror, smiling at it discreetly. She picks up her key-ring and handbag, then disappears.

Nicolas Vanesse is at the checkroom of the Hotel Fønix; he identifies his bags and Sylvie's. The porter checks the numbers on the tags.

NICOLAS

No, not that one.

PORTER

What shall I do with it?

NICOLAS

All right, take them all up to my room.

Dissolve: Nicolas is putting the suitcases, Sylvie's and his, at the back of a large cupboard. He dries himself with a towel and begins to dress. Closeup of Nicolas knotting his tie in front of a mirror. The frame is tightened on his expression. The camera draws back to show the bedroom, untidy, articles of clothing on the bed. Nicolas presses his forehead against the mirror in which he was looking at himself a moment ago. He is hardly moving now: just barely breathing. He looks very tired.

(For the brief period that it lasts, the unity of time must be rigorously respected. What is it? Almost nothing, nothing. The unity of time is merely inserted between two dissociative phases without ever stepping over the gulf that takes the place of the present. Do not destroy this rhythm: maintain a prose speed on this external transitional time. The absence of ellipse forces the theme to be contained entirely within the form. In this case, the unity of time can be respected only at the cost of silence.)

Skansen restaurant. Eva Vos and Nicolas at a table facing each other. Tight closeup of Nicolas.

NICOLAS

Sylvie is dead!

Eva Vos stares at Nicolas, thunderstruck. Nicolas begins again, placidly:

NICOLAS

Sylvie is dead!

They are in the main dining room of the Skansen. The waiter comes up to them, order pad and pencil in hand.

NICOLAS

I'll ask you to order for me. I'd like a filet of sole Kristiansand, a bottle of Chablis...

Eva Vos speaks Norwegian to the waiter; she is deeply moved, her lips quivering. The waiter walks away deferentially.

NICOLAS

Sylvie is dead! That's what I told you in the telegram. She fell when we were climbing. We searched for hours. I was in the Norwegian government helicopter myself. We didn't find a single trace. It had been snowing on Spitsbergen for two days. We may even have flown over her body several times, but there was nothing but snow, snow, snow...

The waiter returns, puts down an ice bucket and the bottle of wine.

EVA VOS

He wants to know if he should open it right away.

NICOLAS

Yes, right away.

The waiter does so. There is total silence between Eva Vos and Nicolas. The waiter gives him some wine to taste. Nicolas indicates that he should serve it. The waiter fills both glasses, replaces the cutlery on the table with the appropriate cutlery for fish. He evaporates again.

EVA VOS

I can hardly believe it. Sylvie dead on her wedding trip...It hurts me, inside me. Sylvie...

NICOLAS

Sylvie is dead!

EVA VOS

Are you leaving for Montreal soon?

NICOLAS

In a few days. Our marriage ended in the middle of our wedding trip. It's horrible, it's unfair. Life is abominably unfair.

EVA VOS

How did it happen...the accident?

NICOLAS

I don't have the strength to tell you just now.

    Nicolas looks at Eva Vos, troubled; he stops eating for a moment.

NICOLAS

You're her friend, I'm going to tell you...Sylvie fell into a crevasse; perhaps she was dragged down by all the equipment. I called her name for hours and hours, and all I heard was the echo of my own voice. I was afraid to go near the crevasse where she fell...It's a hole and the edges and bottom are covered with snow...I kept calling her.

    Eva is moved to tears. Nicolas is impassive, hardened, silent. The waiter brings the filets of sole Kristiansand. He serves vegetables to each of them and refills their glasses with wine.


(If silence has a colour, it is black. We hear Eva Vos and Nicolas separating the white flesh of the fish, swallowing it without rhythm, drinking the white wine without ever communicating. Eva Vos looks furtively at Nicolas when she hears him swallow; Nicolas does not look at her. He is concentrating, overwhelmed by an emotional ictus. During this short sequence the cutting from shots that would normally be long to shots that are extremely close, even fragmented, must be obvious. We start with complete characters, finish with high-angle shots of a plate, fragments of jaws, invisible fish heaped onto forks, green bubbles forming on the wine, lowered eyelids. The spectacle is atomized. Even the rapid accumulation of fragments annihilates the whole, rather than revealing its decomposable totality. The viewer who may be distressed by the disintegration of this sequence feels uneasy, for no one is really accustomed to these instantaneous crumblings of reality.)

NICOLAS

You've hardly said a word since we started to eat.

EVA VOS

What can I say?

NICOLAS

Nothing obliges you to speak to me. You're right.

Nicolas gestures to the waiter, indicates that they have finished. The waiter clears the table.

NICOLAS

Two coffees, an Aquavit...

Nicolas is nervous. He is trembling. Tight closeup of Nicolas.

NICOLAS

You're positive that I've lied to you about Sylvie's accident!

Very tight closeup of Eva. She blinks, mechanically replaces a lock of her brown hair.

EVA VOS

Then what happened?

NICOLAS

I guessed right. So that's it!

EVA VOS

But have you guessed everything?

NICOLAS

What difference does it make? For the past few minutes you've been certain I was lying and you've kept quiet. Why? Why?

EVA

Because I'm afraid of you.

> The waiter arrives with a tray: coffee, a bottle of Aquavit, a glass. He leaves. Nicolas bursts into tears. He sobs noisily. The customers at neighbouring tables turn towards Eva Vos and Nicolas; he wipes his eyes with his napkin. He gets up abruptly, walks across the large dining room to the washroom. The camera comes back to a medium shot of Eva, sitting tensely on her chair. The customers at the neighbouring tables turn around occasionally to glance at her; her beauty probably attracts as many looks as what has just happened between her and her guest. After a brief eclipse Nicolas comes back to the table. His expression is one of gravity and pain. He sits down.

NICOLAS

So you think I killed Sylvie...

EVA VOS

Yes.

NICOLAS

...that I brought her to Norway, on her wedding trip, with that in mind...It's dreadful to think that of me. And it's unfair!

> Nicolas stops, noticing that the other customers in the restaurant are still looking at him and Eva Vos, then he begins again, speaking more softly. Tight closeup of Nicolas: stay on him until the end of his speech.

NICOLAS

You're on the wrong track. Sylvie's death is going to affect all my future existence; it was the worst thing that could happen to me, the most unimaginable...Sylvie is dead. She killed herself before my eyes.

EVA VOS

What?!!!

NICOLAS

You can't invent a thing like that. She was ahead of me, close to me, we were alone in the world and she took her own life.

103

I don't think I'll ever have the courage to tell anyone the truth when I get back to Montreal. People will think what you did, that I killed her! You're the first person I've told about Sylvie's death, and you seek out my murderer's hands, my killer's expression...with absolute certainty!

Nicolas hides his face in his hands.

EVA VOS

Nicolas...Forgive me, I beg you.

Nicolas gestures to the waiter to bring the bill.

EVA

Let's get out of here. It's suffocating, and I'm very upset by these people craning their necks to look at us.

NICOLAS

Go outside and wait for me, at the door; I'll be right back.

EVA

What did you tell the police in Svalbard?

NICOLAS

I lied. But the climbing accident didn't seem suspicious to them, I don't think.

EVA

What if they find Sylvie's body?

NICOLAS

Under the snow? Impossible. Next year she'll be buried under an even thicker layer and it will go on like that, year after year.

EVA

You must always be on guard against the investigators' per-. severance.

NICOLAS

There's nothing to be afraid of.

The waiter brings the bill. Nicolas pays. Eva and Nicolas head for the exit. Exterior travelling shot. Eva and Nicolas walk a few steps without saying anything. The day is hot. Eva leads Nicolas towards the Askershus citadel. Nicolas takes off his sports jacket. They walk slowly because of the steep grade. The overwhelming fortress of the Askershus is built on a promontory, according to classic strategic precepts: the ground itself constitutes the citadel's natural first floor. Eva walks along the ramparts which look down on Oslo and its fjord. A string of dendrites reminds the inattentive walkers that they are wandering through a product of war. Eva sits in an embrasure, Nicolas stands beside her. She turns her back to the bay and looks at Nicolas. From Eva's point of view Nicolas' brown hair blends with the upper towers of the Askershus, broken by small embrasures. Subjective camera. Encircling low-angle shot of Nicolas, encircling because it is constantly moving. His shadowed eyes look like two wells of mourning. Reverse shot: Eva's furtive looks, her expression of gentleness and *loaengsel*.

NICOLAS
It's as though life has deserted me.

Nicolas stops short and walks back down.

NICOLAS
Let's forget about this walk; I'm going back to the hotel.

Eva follows him. They walk down to the city in silence; the heat is intense.

Dissolve. Eva and Nicolas are motionless, on the sidewalk of a street flanked by two rows of buildings in incarnate brick. Insert flashes: Sylvie in medium closeup. The scene is cabin 9 on the *Nordnorge*. Sylvie is naked, moving frenetically above Nicolas' body.

The incarnate bricks are a reminder of all that has touched Sylvie's skin, of dragon's blood as red as her own. Incarnation refers to death, the beginning to its end, revealing through this circularity the veiled structure of the film.

NICOLAS

Suddenly she started running ahead of me, across the hard snow...and she literally plunged into the precipice.

EVA

She didn't say anything?

NICOLAS

Nothing.

> Nicolas wipes his forehead. Medium shot of Eva who is looking at him. In perspective, the red brick buildings.

EVA

We've lost Sylvie, both of us.

NICOLAS

Forget Sylvie! I can't forgive her for what she did.

> Nicolas runs away from Eva. Eva, surprised, watches him move away and disappear. Series of dissolves of Eva: she walks, stops, looks behind her, around her; she advances like a sleepwalker.

(I was not, I have been, I remember, I no longer am...Eva's steps are only the modalities of her movement; even frozen on the screen in closeup, Eva continues to stir, for even if she is no longer moving, if she stops dead, the viewer carries on. Despite Sylvie's glorious spasms on the screen, she is not moving, she no longer moves. She was not, she has been, she no longer is, she will no longer be.)

> Night. Nicolas has a view of the city from the window of his ninth-floor room in the Fønix. Garlands of lights criss-cross and follow the city's thoroughfares. The air is very hot.

NICOLAS

This afternoon, on the Askershus, I didn't want the day to end. There was just one thing in my mind: to do what Sylvie did.

Swish pan to Eva, sitting in an easy chair: she is barefoot, rubbing her ankles. In front of her, on a lowboy table, there is a platter of smørbrød and a bottle of Rhine wine, almost empty.

EVA

And now...?

Medium shot of Nicolas who turns towards Eva. He comes over to the table, sits on the floor.

NICOLAS

Things have changed.

Nicolas goes on eating and drinking. Eva puts her shoes on.

EVA

It's getting late.

NICOLAS

Are you leaving right away?

EVA

Yes. I'm going back.

NICOLAS

Is someone expecting you?

EVA

I live alone. I go back to work at nine o'clock tomorrow morning. And I have to get some sleep.

NICOLAS

What time is it?

EVA

After eleven.

NICOLAS

Think of me as a brother, all right? And I'll treat you as though you were my sister.

EVA

I'll stay.

> They continue eating. Eva is all softness; her eyes are flush with her face. *Loaengsel* again, that profound yearning of the soul – but for what? Nicolas is bare-chested. Eva has taken her shoes off. She lies on the bed, on her left side; she looks at Nicolas.

EVA

May I?

NICOLAS

Yes, of course.

> Subjective camera, Eva's point of view: slanted shot of Nicolas. He gets up, turns off the overhead lights. The ceiling light in the hallway illuminates the room a little. He goes back to the window.

NICOLAS

Natchez-under-the-Hill...does that mean anything to you?

EVA

Natchez... Yes, vaguely. Sylvie talked to me about Natchez, but I don't remember any more than that.

NICOLAS

Try to remember, Eva.

> From the window, Nicolas looks towards the bed without distinguishing Eva's features.

EVA

Why are you talking to me about Natchez? Are you trying to shed light on some mystery?

NICOLAS

Perhaps; but perhaps I'm also just trying to make you talk about anything at all so the night will pass unnoticed.

Dissolve: Nicolas standing at the bathroom mirror.

NICOLAS

How do you say *chagrin* in Norwegian?

> Eva does not reply. Nicolas walks about, sits on the edge of the bed, facing Eva.

EVA

In Norwegian we say melancholy...

> Nicolas stretches out beside Eva on the bed. They are side by side but their bodies do not touch; this strange couple radiates calm.

NICOLAS

You say melancholy, just like in French?

EVA

Melancholy, like in French...

NICOLAS

In that case, Eva, you don't have muscles of chagrin, you have muscles of melancholy.

EVA

What's that, muscles of melancholy?

> Nicolas turns towards Eva, puts two fingers in the middle of her forehead and pulls the skin towards the top. Eva's eyebrows form a circumflex accent with the point in the middle of her forehead.

NICOLAS

Sylvie had remarkable muscles of chagrin. When she had that expression I was completely bowled over. It happened when she was finding life too painful. It's the image of her that I'll always remember.

EVA

I never saw her sad. On the contrary, she was radiant. Of course I only stayed in Montreal for six weeks.

NICOLAS

Is Oslo always this hot in the summer?

EVA

Very hot and humid...like Montreal.

> A long silence. They are lying on their backs, symmetrical.

EVA

Are we still brother and sister?

NICOLAS

Yes.

EVA

I'm going to take off my suit; it's too hot.

> Eva gets up, takes off her white suit and hangs it in the hallway. She comes back to the bed, wearing just her sky-blue underwear. She lies down again. Eva and Nicolas look in each other's eyes, silent, for a long time.

EVA

I can't see the colour of your eyes; everything is dark.

NICOLAS

Blue.

EVA

It's so strange, the two of us together here like this. Right here, in my country, and after everything that's happened.

> Eva and Nicolas are lying on the bed, parallel, close to each other and not touching, in peaceful intimacy.

NICOLAS

I'll never be able to love again...

> Eva turns her head towards him, taking care not to encroach on the space between them. Nicolas has closed his eyes. Shot of the bed with the two recumbent figures on it.

(Until this point in the film we might say that Quebec is in a void. Its recurrent eclipse makes one think of the absence of a presence, of an incomplete mystery...)

Same room. The following night. Eva and Nicolas are wearing the same clothes.

EVA

Last night I watched you fall asleep...and you talked.

NICOLAS

What did I say?

EVA

I'll never be able to love again...

They are leaning on the narrow balcony outside the window.

EVA

I wasn't very enthusiastic at the office today. Anyway, I can delegate my work to others because I'm leaving in three weeks.

NICOLAS

I think it's even hotter than it was last night.

EVA

There isn't any breeze.

Eva takes a few steps towards the room. Nicolas goes inside too. Alternate closeups of Nicolas and Eva; we hear Eva's voice over a shot of Nicolas.

EVA

I'm not your sister, you're not my brother.

Nicolas crushes Eva against the wall, near the window. He opens Eva's lips with his tongue. He thrusts his right hand between her legs with a suddenness that is almost brutal. Eva has unfastened her brassiere which falls between their bodies. They lie on the rug, Eva on her back, looking into Nicolas' eyes. He caresses Eva's breasts, twists her nipples cruelly between his index and middle fingers. She spreads her legs, Nicolas enters her. Carried away by an unquenchable haste they cling to each other. The darkness becomes silent, the silence opaque.

Dissolve: we can make out the entwined couple, their bodies barely separated, at rest.

NICOLAS

No one knows anyone...

EVA

Why do you say that?

Nicolas looks at Eva who kisses him avidly on the stomach, the chest, the neck.

NICOLAS

I didn't know Sylvie.

Eva continues to cover him with kisses on the chest, the arms, under the arms. She begins once more as though the storm which has just abated were rising again. Nicolas lets himself be enveloped by Eva's lips. His expression is one of absence and repose.

NICOLAS

No one knows anyone...

We see Eva's profile and her open mouth: other kisses make her move out of the tight frame. Closeup of Nicolas. Superimposed on Nicolas' iris, Eva strolling along Lille Grensen. As she approaches the camera lens, optical pulsations distort the image and give it an oneiric cadence.

NICOLAS    (out of frame)

No one knows anyone...

The focal pulsations of the image make Eva move away from the camera and come closer to it. She is wearing a tussore dress that comes to mid-thigh, revealing her svelteness. Eva's dark hair sets her apart from the great majority of the people in Oslo with whom she comes into contact on Lille Grensen and who, like her, are clinging to the shop windows. Medium shot of Nicolas inside one of these shops. He sees Eva coming, but does not reveal himself; she walks past him, right under his eyes, not knowing that she is being observed by the very person she is going to meet on a terrace of the Studenterlunden.

(When we see Eva on the Lille Grensen, the film's musical theme is introduced. This musical blossoming is accompanied by the image of Eva. Suddenly the image is no more than the response to an off-camera music whose supremacy is artful. Generally, when the music in a film is subdued the film is almost without music; but here, when the music bursts out it becomes supreme. It is the masque of which the visual representations of Eva represent the antimasque. The music in the film arises from its visual content: it precedes but does not accompany it. Eva, the antimasque, only makes the orphic hymn which is dedicated to her extend onto Lille Grensen. The way she moves, her graceful walk, the beauty of her motions refer the viewer to the invisible stretto underlying all these visual insertions. The film is interiorized during this passage on the Lille Grensen. When Eva's masque is dropped the film begins again. It is important in this passage to let the image flow, not compose it too much, leave it partly undetermined, so that the weight of the music is not contested by any detail of the visual treatment and so that the viewer, already sensitized to the impromptu nature of the image, is in a better position to appreciate the other score.)

Direct cut to Eva sitting at a table on the terrace of a café in the Studenterlunden. Camera subjective from Nicolas' point of view. Eva, smiling, arranges a lock of

113

hair; she puts her elbows on the table and looks at Nicolas, dazzled, grateful, radiant. Optical pulsations begin to dilate and contract the image at a slightly diminished rhythm. Eva's face is composed and disappears into a genesis that keeps beginning again, but is never completed.

EVA

Do I have muscles of chagrin too?

Nicolas does not reply; he raises his head, smiles, takes one of Eva's hands in his own.

EVA

What did you do today?

NICOLAS

I worked on my screenplay.

EVA

Your screenplay?

NICOLAS

The film I told you about.

The waiter arrives.

NICOLAS

A double Chivas Regal – two!

EVA

Your screenplay, I know; you told me you didn't want to talk about it.

NICOLAS

I hadn't envisaged a Norwegian woman of your age, who resembles you, or Sylvie's death...or this intrusion of reality into the imaginary.

EVA

So the film is autobiographical, then?

NICOLAS

If you want...I haven't found a better way to do it. But my

autobiography goes considerably beyond the fiction I thought I was unable to invent.

In a surprising and truly incongruous move, Nicolas sticks his hand inside Eva's blouse. The people near them seem not to notice this audacious behaviour by Nicolas, whose wrist seems grafted to Eva's bosom. The camera focuses on Nicolas' frenzied expression.

EVA

You're hurting me a little.

Direct cut to a closeup of Sylvie, her expression pleading. Reverse shot: Nicolas, pained by Sylvie's return into the texture of the present, withdraws his hand and looks at it.

NICOLAS

Please forgive me, Eva.

EVA

What for?

NICOLAS

You were right to tell me I was hurting you.

EVA

What are you talking about? I didn't say anything.

Nicolas looks into Eva's eyes with terror.

NICOLAS

I've written a rough draft. After I left Montreal I just added some notes and glosses to my synopsis.

EVA

You must know the broad outlines of the story already?

NICOLAS

Of course.

The same scene that took place earlier is repeated. Nicolas sticks his hand into Eva's blouse and rubs her breast, taking it out of its lacy envelope. With the tip of his thumb Nicolas makes the nipple stand out, be re-absorbed, come out again. Close shot of Nicolas: he is staring and his face is the ascetic, even painful mask of ecstasy.

EVA

You're hurting me a little.

Flash closeup of Sylvie, open-mouthed, stupefied, horrified. Series of shots of Nicolas: he goes on caressing Eva's breast with obsessive regularity. They are still sitting at the table on the terrace of the café in the Studenterlunden. The camera moves back. Cut.

Closeup of Nicolas, eyes closed; he is tossing painfully, victim of an inner fever or a nightmare. The camera dollies back to reveal the set: Eva and Nicolas are lying in the room at the Fønix Hotel. Nicolas emits formless moans as though he were being tortured with a blow-torch. Eva gets out of bed, tries to wake Nicolas by shaking his shoulders, but he struggles furiously. Eva turns on the bedside lamp, places it just under Nicolas' eyes. Nicolas immediately opens his eyes, sits up and tries to determine where he is. Eva is sitting close to him, loving and concerned.

EVA

You had a nightmare, Nicolas. You were screaming...Look: you're covered with sweat.

Eva's breasts are bare. She gets up, brings him a bath-towel, wipes his forehead, face and chest.

NICOLAS

Hamlet...

EVA

Don't move, I'll bring you a glass of cold water.

Eva hurries away and comes back with a large glass of cold water. Nicolas drinks it down in one motion.

116

NICOLAS

I was playing Hamlet in an Italian city on the edge of the Barents Sea.

EVA

Nicolas, Nicolas...

NICOLAS

I was terrified; I couldn't finish the production. I remember, with sorrow, the illuminated theatre.

EVA

Calm yourself, Nicolas... You still haven't got over your nightmare.

He looks into her eyes, surprised. He touches her brown hair, her breasts that are offered to him, her face.

NICOLAS

You know Eva, you can't get to Svalbard from that Italian enclave in the far north. There are no air or sea connections with Longyearbyen or Ny Ålesund.

EVA

Forget about the Italian enclave. There's no Italian enclave inside the Arctic Circle.

NICOLAS

I know what you're going to tell me – that I'm delirious, that the Italian enclave on the shore of the Barents Sea has never existed, that I've invented everything.

EVA

Yes, that's exactly what I'm going to tell you. At least admit that you haven't got over your bad dream yet.

NICOLAS

The city was built according to a concentric plan. The avenues come out of the centre like radii, the streets are circular and cut across the avenues. The central area is a masterpiece.

EVA

Nicolas, stop. There's no Italian city in Lapland, I'm positive.

117

The big Milan stores have luxurious branches there.

Eva takes him by the shoulders and shakes him vigor-
ously.

I'm finding it harder and harder to understand why you're
trying to make me doubt something that exists. That illuminated theatre... Those beautiful snow-covered avenues... You
can't know.


(Nicolas' oneiric stubbornness could seem as gratuitous as
the illuminated theatre he has just mentioned for the second
time. We do not know whether its interior or exterior is illuminated, if this stubbornness didn't give the more or less inattentive viewer a very clear indication that the Svalbard
archipelago where Sylvie Dubuque and Nicolas Vanesse
went on their wedding trip does not exist. Cooped up in the
darkness of the cinema, engaged in a movement that no
longer depends on him, the viewer cannot interrupt the projection for a few minutes in order to consult an atlas or the
Montreal consular guide. But here we are in the middle of the
Oslo night; and while Nicolas is coming out of a nightmare
the viewer begins to believe no more than Eva does in the
existence of an Italian enclave looking out on the Barents
Sea and [this borders on self-mutilation], to doubt the existence of the Svalbard archipelago which the film-maker has
completely fabricated so as to have the action take place
there. After all, we don't stick Alps in the middle of the
Arctic Ocean, any more than we build a Renaissance set in
Lapland. After Nicolas' nightmare the viewer capitulates and
consents *illico* to give the Svalbard archipelago back to the
film-maker, with its cardboard villages and fantastic glaciers;
it is also possible that long before this treatment he had de-
tected some similarities between the glacial lace of Isfjorden
and the invaginated frontispieces of the Alaskan littoral, between the crests of Cape Mitra and the basaltic hair of the

Sverdrup islands, between the configuration of Kongsfjorden and that of Repulse Bay...Nothing is more corrosive than doubt. The Italian enclave leads to the artificiality of Spitsbergen which leads, by induction, to the crevassed massifs of Alaska, stuck in the Barents Sea by a delirious cartographer...Nicolas' nightmare spreads by shocks that cause the entire set of the film to tremble, but still do not free it from its burden of sorrow and desolation. Uninhabited, the set becomes insidiously taxed with unreality and, through a mirror effect of Nicolas' nightmare, this set becomes transparent to the extent that its usurped identity can be guessed at and, for viewers who have been warned, it is now only the other side of the picture. Spitsbergen dissolves and drifts from east to west beneath the solid ice-pack. Doubt is an endomorphosis; and the present official statement does not stop its movement.)

The room at the Fønix Hotel, dimly lit. Nicolas is working in an armchair near the window. Night.

EVA

And afterwards?

NICOLAS

I don't know what will come afterwards.

EVA

You stopped at Sylvie's death?

NICOLAS

No, just after. I stopped at you, when you burst into my life, those nights we spent together in Oslo.

EVA

Why must your film be autobiographical?

NICOLAS

I don't know. It's only autobiographical from my point of view. Anyone who can say that it's autobiographical already knows me. The public can never know for sure if such a work is autobiographical or not. Autobiography is a false category.

EVA

The film tells the story of an actor who leaves the business to make a film which will be an account of his life from that moment. It's like a film within a film – "the play within the play" – like in Hamlet.

NICOLAS

No...Hamlet invented the strategy of the play to catch Claudius. In my screenplay the fiction isn't a trap; it's the fiction that is trapped by a reality it didn't contain and which hypocritically invades it.

Eva has approached Nicolas. She strokes the back of his neck as he speaks. Nicolas is still holding his large black notebook; he flips through it.

NICOLAS

No one will ever be able to say that my film is autobiographical.

EVA

Except me?

NICOLAS

Except you, Eva. But if the film is autobiographical it must be so completely. After the funereal wedding trip the story changes tone. Sylvie's death has disturbed the course of my life...and of the film. Then a Norwegian woman who resembles you appears in the unfinished text of the screenplay. She is part of the film too.

EVA

I'm not an actress.

NICOLAS

I'm not a film-maker yet.

EVA

You'll find an actress who looks like me.

NICOLAS

I know. Actors play false: they've been taught to confuse the natural and the parodical so well that they can do no better than be natural when they're playing a parody and vice versa...I know something about that.

EVA

But you'll need people to play the parts.

NICOLAS

Yes. And you to play the part of Eva Vos, shoot this scene in this room, in the middle of the night.

EVA

Am I an important character in your film?

NICOLAS

I don't know; I write the screenplay as I live it. And I haven't finished living it, so the screenplay is incomplete.

> They are lying on the bed. Nicolas puts his mouth on Eva's breasts. Eva moans a little, but Nicolas continues and at the same time prods her between her legs. Eva writhes, then convulsive movements make her arch her body in the midst of the sheets and pillows. Then she lies flat on her back while Nicolas performs an *irrumatio* that welds their bodies to each other and kneads them into one clay. The sequence of shots gives the effect of a centrifugal spiral which mixes Eva's hair with Nicolas' pubic hair and causes Nicolas' head to be lost in Eva's open thighs. A single body shaken from within is dying in triumphal solitude and unity.

(Tomorrow springs from memory. There have been tomorrows, but can one know whether they will extend into yesterday? Tomorrow is only a shadow of yesterday. Everything splits. Nothing escapes this implacable law. Time itself, fluid fluid, is but a sponge soiled by all the ventures it seems to encourage and then buries, one after the other, in a single bath of sorrow. Time is a pregnant virgin. And if it is a river, that river is a swift cemetery which carries everything away, even the shores that border it and the ships that float on its surface! Film, better than any other means of expression, renders this Acherontic fluidity, at least to the extent that it never stops before the end of its own projection. Everything is bound together. When all's said and done the viewer is in the presence of an endless image, inside which discontinuities are included through some process of abruption. The duration of each shot coincides with the duration of its projection, but the viewer never perceives when one frame is substituted for another. Thus, twenty-four images per second are able to feed the pigmentary epithelium enough so that the viewer perceives neither the rivets nor the blades of the shutter. This nyctalopic powder is put into the viewer's brain and enables him to reconstitute the river of time that leads us all to death.)

3:30 p.m. Everything is slashed with sun. The taxi takes off like a whirlwind, makes its way easily onto the cloverleaf next to the airport at Dorval. The taxi heads east towards Montreal along highway 40. Nicolas throws his head back on the seat and dozes.

Dissolve to the cabin of the helicopter flying over the mountains and glaciers beside the Magdalenefjorden. Everyone in the machine is asking Nicolas for a sign, some indication, but he has lost control of himself and he is looking desperately in every direction. The noise of the rotor drowns the other voices; Nicolas, isolated in his silence, seems absent. The helicopter grazes the rocky ridges, flies dangerously close to the spurs and turrets which can be discerned under the roofs of snow like the tips of girders. High-angle shots: the camera looks over the motionless rivers and climbs up epiglacial valleys. Then, a half-turn: descend where the camera has already climbed, cling too closely to the powdery slopes, just avoid cutting the ice with the knife. Make the camera vomitive. Nicolas' taxi ride, a veritable nightmare, is taking place in the helicopter and the damp heat of Montreal seems to be emanating from the *inlandsis* of Spitsbergen. The shots accentuate the dangerous nature of the Norwegian government helicopter's manoeuvres: it moves through valleys hemmed in by enormous shoulders and takes on the shape of the slightest depression in the plateaus. Medium shot of Nicolas asleep in the taxi: through the window we can see how fast the taxi is travelling along the Décarie expressway. Suddenly, the landscape seen through the rear-view mirror begins to dance and sway and the viewer realizes that the driver has lost control of his car. Flashes of the helicopter flying above the Magdalene-fjorden. The shot tightens on a closeup of Nicolas, still asleep. The noise of a violent collision and the car being shaken pull him out of his sleep: he opens his eyes, immediately covers his face to protect himself. Five or six cars are involved in a multiple collision. There is an explosion nearby. The bodies of the cars shatter. Nicolas is thrown to the opposite side of the seat. We hear cries of panic or pain. Cut.

(According to the unwritten laws of dramaturgy, accidents must always take place within the internal coherence of the action. They must be necessary or meaningful. This accident represents neither fate nor punishment; it has no privileged dimension: dramatically speaking, it is empty, not pertinent to the screenplay. Its occurrence is nothing more than aleatory. This aspect is reinforced to some extent by the fact that Nicolas does not come out of it crippled. He has only a fractured scaphoid bone in his left hand.)

Nicolas is getting out at the Voyageur bus station in Black Lake, a small village in the Eastern Townships of

Quebec which must be satisfied with gigantic slag-heaps by way of landscape. Charlotte, Sylvie's older sister, is waiting for him at the station. Very long shots: we see Charlotte and Nicolas embracing, then getting into a Pontiac station-wagon. Travelling shot. The Pontiac pulls out of the terminal, leaves the downtown area and drives through a nicely landscaped suburb with rows of large, spacious houses. The car enters the driveway beside one of these residences. Inside the car.

NICOLAS

And Denis?

CHARLOTTE

He never gets back from the office before six.

Charlotte is several months pregnant; she is pretty, even seductive, but bears very little resemblance to her younger sister. Shots inside the house.

CHARLOTTE

Tell me...

Shots of Nicolas; the cast on his left wrist is bothering him. He looks at Charlotte, saying nothing.

Insert flashes of Sylvie on the *Nordnorge*, astride Nicolas. These flashes establish an atmosphere of fascination between Charlotte and Nicolas.

CHARLOTTE

What are you saying? She fell! But were you so far away from her that you couldn't hold her back?

Medium shot of Sylvie, seated goddess reigning over Nicolas: she has her orgasm.

Closeup of Charlotte.

CHARLOTTE

What will you have to drink – scotch or vodka?

NICOLAS

Scotch and water.

Charlotte pours his drink; she holds out a glass half-filled with Chivas Regal.

NICOLAS
Aren't you drinking, Charlotte?

CHARLOTTE
Just orange juice, for love of my child.

NICOLAS
I'm beat.

CHARLOTTE
The guest room's ready for you. Does your wrist hurt very much?

NICOLAS
It's bearable. You didn't tell your mother about Sylvie?

CHARLOTTE
She's still in that psychiatric hospital in Winnipeg.

NICOLAS
And how about your father?

CHARLOTTE
Denis doesn't want me to tell him. He's going to take care of it himself. He's still very angry at my father. I don't think he'll ever forgive him for never coming to Black Lake, not once, to see us. You've never met him, of course?

NICOLAS
Your father was in Europe on business when we got married.

Church of Saint Suzanne in Black Lake. The priest is finishing the office in front of the place where the coffin is usually placed.

PRIEST
Death comes slowly for those who have found the light. Sylvie Vanesse, you were blinded by the light. And now you have left us for a kingdom where all is diaphanous. Where you are, nothing is opaque, and light encounters light. Let all

125

men raise their thoughts towards God whose world is but an answer. They shall recognize in him the master whose name is plentitude...I am Alpha and Omega.

The priest meditates silently. Charlotte, Denis and Nicolas do the same. Charlotte suddenly bursts into tears; Denis takes her arm and leads her away.

Exterior. In front of the church. The day is hot and particularly beautiful. Denis is leading his wife to the car; Nicolas sits on the middle seat of the Pontiac station-wagon. At the end of the main street in Black Lake the car takes a number of turns, then enters the suburb where Denis and Charlotte live.

Dissolve to a shot of the three eating a sandwich lunch in the garden.

CHARLOTTE
You weren't my brother-in-law for very long, Nicolas.

NICOLAS
No, that's true.

CHARLOTTE
Poor Sylvie! Now that she's dead I feel guilty for not having been more present in her life.

Closeup of Charlotte watching Nicolas, weeping. Flashes of Sylvie astride Nicolas. Alternate with her sister's face streaming with tears. For shots of Sylvie at the peak of her orgasm, substitute moving shots of the white precipices of Spitsbergen. Thus Charlotte's face alternates with white images on which we can discern curtains of ice, spots of fahlbende and eyed gneiss.

End on a shot of a layer of snow that is suddenly transformed into a vitrified black texture. After about twenty seconds, make this black glass explode. Sylvie's pendant passes through the glass, leaving a necklace of shards around its rim. The pendant strikes again and makes part of what was left burst into splinters. The image goes out of focus so that the viewer does not see where the blow is coming from. The pendant strikes once again and causes the last fragments of the glass to volatilize. Sylvie appears in the background. Low-angle shot of her wearing only her underpants and brassiere, one knee on the bed; with her right arm she brings her pendant into the centre of the frame. Next shot: frame by frame, we see the pendant, at the end of its chain, gradually approach the centre of the screen. We see Sylvie's face and the spark of fury in her expression. The shot freezes on the hyacinth of Compostela in the middle of the metallic intaglio.

Nicolas throws himself on his side to avoid the blow aimed at his penis. He is horrified; blood is pouring over his hands and thighs.

NICOLAS

Sylvie, I beg you, stop! No, Sylvie, no, no!!!

Nicolas, obviously somnambulistic, stumbles against a piece of furniture and falls. He switches on a lamp: he looks stupefied, like a passenger who has just fallen on the ballast, thinking he has slipped into his bunk. Nicolas looks at his cast. He is bathed in sweat. He has trouble breathing; it is the middle of the night. He gets up, goes to his work-table. He opens the black notebook on the blotting pad and begins to write without interruption.

NICOLAS

The difficulty of transposing this nightmare comes from the absence of spatial references; it's as though the bad dream had only occurred in a temporal register: night, the brevity of the abysmal flashes, the time of the fall, the time for regaining consciousness and the time it took to return to Black Lake. Is there only one lake at Black Lake? The space of the nightmare is as black as the stained glass window that filtered the immaculate snow of Spitsbergen just before Sylvie's pendant pulverized it... The dark space has no depth, no movement (for who could discern it unless a fall were to break its homogeneity?). Starting now, break the silence about Fortinbras, who from the beginning has given the impression of being a rejected hero. Thus we must find a propitious opportunity for the gradual unveiling of the story of Fortinbras, which illuminates with disturbing light the system of symbols in the tragedy of Hamlet, Prince of Denmark. Because Hamlet will be shown on television in two weeks, it is most appropriate to postpone the solution of the puzzle until then. If Eva comes she will be able to see me on television, in the costume of the prince of Norway. Consider, of course, inserting this performance of Hamlet and its commentary into the screenplay. After all, the reflexiveness of the film should not trouble the viewer. On the contrary, there is a good chance that it will satisfy him, for he will find himself in the presence of not just one story but a second one as well, and a commentary on the two plots. I am being overcome by fatigue again and I hope that this time it will induce me into a sleep that will be safe from any nightmare....Even this text that I'm preparing to finish is part of my screenplay.


(Throughout this written text keep the camera frozen on Nicolas; disconcert the viewer to some extent – he is expecting inset flashes or visual metonymies of Nicolas' handwritten text. That would be too facile. What is needed at this point in the film is precisely for the viewer to accept everything, so that he himself will discover in this gentle resignation the justification for what he is so avidly looking at . He knows, even confusedly, that he belongs to the film, just as it, in uneven reciprocity, belongs to him and cannot escape him. This confidence on the part of the viewer is a fundamental condition for exchange; the viewer knows that the film cannot profit from a safe-conduct or from the immunity generally accorded hermetic poems. The seed of the film may not germinate instantaneously but it is, at once and in a single transactional present, transmitted to the cortical centres of vision and to the capsular tissue of the intelligence.

The present, which has been employed from the outset, is the time of the screenplay because it does not relate anything, but transmits an intention – and not just any intention: an abduction! The account of a picturesque rape is rather washed-out if we compare it with a planned rape; a plan always transcends its past definite. That goes without saying; but what is less obvious is the relationship between this violent terminology and the situation of the viewer at the film. How to make explicit, in fact, that the viewer's passivity is more like a devouring passivity than the stoical indifference of frigidity? Perhaps this analogy will still be unproven when the film is over, but its powers of persuasion profit from its implicit nature. Perhaps the viewer will suddenly be offended when he realizes that he has done everything to be raped, offended, too, when he deduces that the spectacle he is watching is hypocritically entering him to the point where he becomes, in spite of himself no doubt, a bearer of van Leeuwenhoek's indivisible animalcules, which have complied with theoretical existence only through optical processes. Of course the viewer hesitates to perceive himself as a succubus when he is sunk in the obscurity of a movie theatre, and to admit the troubled complementarity of the film and of the person who watches it right to the end. Something hard to admit is linked to any freely consented obscurity, even that of a cinema, and for that very reason people should wear masks to the cinema. Because the actors appear barefaced, it is up to the viewers to adopt this outdated usage for their own benefit, and by so doing to confer a new dimension on the act of looking and listening. Masked viewers would experience more profoundly and more freely what their neighbours' presence in the theatre transforms into a too highly codified ceremony. The mask, face of pure conformity, would have the effect of completely freeing the viewer, freeing him from the constraints of his identity, sparing him from hiding his joy or feigning his emotions and accustoming himself to the intoxicating intensity of what he himself has lived. The ideal would be to imagine the reader of a book wearing a mask which he might even use as a signet. How to show these reflections in a film? Don't think about it.)

Hotel Sonesta, room 1001. Night. Nicolas is sitting at a desk, writing in his big black notebook, while Eva is sleeping soundly in the semi-darkness. Nicolas is filling the black notebook that he had in Oslo with a slanting handwriting, difficult to decipher. He seems to be concentrating particularly hard; he stops, drinks some Chivas Regal, gets up, paces the room, looks at Eva sleeping, curled up. He walks over to the bay window that looks over downtown Montreal and its fringe of lighted skyscrapers, then goes back to work. He dives into the black notebook and rereads some passages. He has all sorts of nervous habits as he works: he rumples his hair, rubs his cast against his left thigh, scraping it. He keeps looking at himself in the dresser mirror; when he leans back in the chair he catches sight of Eva in another mirror. He utters some words, as though articulating in silence might finally inspire him with what he is preparing to write. Next to the notebook are some loose sheets on which he draws scrolls, love-knots, spirals. There is obviously no relationship between these graphic outlets and Nicolas' screenplay.

He glances at the bed in the mirror which serves as a rear-view mirror and sees a silent, distressing image. Sylvie is masturbating with great frenzy, stopping suddenly with an expression of joy and delight. Closeup of Nicolas: he is upset. He draws compulsively, then slips his pen between the cast and his left arm to scratch it.

Dissolve: Nicolas is lying on the floor, his black notebook and loose sheets of paper all around him. He is fast asleep, head against the rug.

Dissolve: Outside. Day. Nicolas wakes up, cursing the light, which is blinding him. He looks at his untidy papers, then at the bed. Eva is not there. Nicolas goes into the bathroom. He does not even notice Eva's return;

130

she knocks tactfully on the bathroom door.

EVA

Aren't you going to kiss me?

His face is covered with shaving cream. She is smiling.

EVA

Did you work all night again? Go on, I'll watch you. Nicolas, I've made a decision. We're going to leave the hotel today. I've had enough of this kind of life. I've been in Montreal for four days now but I feel as though I'm living artificially. You didn't want me to live in your apartment out of respect for my feelings...because of Sylvie.

NICOLAS

What are you getting at?

EVA

Don't be so defensive. I read your screenplay when I got up this morning. The last pages especially...Anyway, didn't you tell me yesterday that you'd let me read it one of these days?

Nicolas cuts his chin; he immediately takes the cover off his styptic pencil, wets it and applies it several times to the cut.

NICOLAS

I don't see how you could have read that in my screenplay!

EVA

Let's say I interpreted, that's all. There's one thing I want to tell you: it won't bother me to live in Sylvie's apartment, in her place! I was her friend...and even though she's dead I still love her. My bags are all ready.

Eva inspects the cupboards, the drawers. She collects Nicolas' clothes and puts them on the bed. Nicolas comes out of the bathroom.

EVA

You've got circles under your eyes, Nicolas.

131

NICOLAS

The worst thing is I'm not making any progress with my screenplay. I've got a block.

EVA

Why?

NICOLAS

I don't know.

EVA

That shouldn't be happening, because you're writing the screenplay as you live it. As far as I can tell you haven't stopped living since Oslo.

Eva puts Nicolas' shirts in a suitcase.

EVA

Let me do it... You've got enough problems with your cast.

NICOLAS

When did you get up?

EVA

At nine o'clock I were...

NICOLAS

I was.

EVA

At nine o'clock I was all dressed. So I decided to go for a walk along Sherbrooke Street.

NICOLAS

So you just wandered around like that for more than two hours?

EVA

As you can see. Shall I put your books in your attaché case?

NICOLAS

Yes.

Eva packs everything carefully. Nicolas has held onto the black notebook; now he leafs through it, goes back several pages. He stops at a passage. Closeup of Nicolas. Dissolve to black.

Nicolas is standing on a snowy dome on Spitsbergen. The camera shoots him from the front, first in high angle then at his level. Nicolas slowly moves back on his balcony of snow; behind, at the back, a rocky collar closes in the landscape. Nicolas is alone. He walks back slowly, as though executing, backwards, a triumphal entry to the tune of Baldi's *Discorso*. The camera keeps moving forward, Nicolas backwards; the perspective of the mountains is distorted, the notch seems deeper, so deep that this optical metamorphosis might place a crater in front of the mountainous scotia decorating the background, in which Nicolas – whether he knows it or not – is about to throw himself. Closeup of Nicolas. He falls backwards, an expression of terror on his face, and lies in the snow, eyes open. His head is grazing the edge of the precipice.

(At a certain point in the film everything is critical, so nothing more need be decided. The viewer, having let himself be involved from the outset, is suddenly no longer preoccupied with what might happen. Within himself, he knows that the transaction is being performed according to the usual canons; but far from feeling totally involved or constrained to conform to his role of manipulated viewer, he loses interest in what had at first mystified him; he placidly tunes out of a show where he had carved a quasi-privileged place for himself. It's as though a predictable threshold is inevitably incorporated into any structure founded on unpredictability, and the approach of this threshold exhausts the viewer. The film is no longer carrying the viewer forward. It would be unfair to refer only to the viewer's fatigue to explain the attainment of this tonal ceiling; it is, rather, a matter of a phenomenon of entropy. Meaning no longer passes, the film has become unrefractory under the effect of a morbid overheating. This is the threshold of irreversibility of any artistic experiment, the threshold which must be crossed, or the experiment cannot be concluded. This is the nightmare of the unpredictable. There is nothing comparable in literature, because when the reader enters the zone of entropy he has only to put the book on a table, simply perform a salutary cooling operation that will allow him to begin again later. The film viewer cannot stop the projection, stick a marker on the sequence that is growing opaque and go and amuse himself for a few minutes, hoping that meanwhile the entropy will lift, like fog. No, that can't be done. The film goes on, the viewer too; and the slowdown in communication must, if possible sort itself out without interrupting the show or starting it again. The unpredictable must reestablish its hold in such a way that the spectator escapes the attrition that was beginning and feels that he is once again engaged in a chain of unpredictability. Instead of trying to foresee what he is expecting [which generally leads to bankruptcy], he must expect what he does not want to predict, endlessly metamorphosing the unpredictable into the unpredicted, and his faculty for prediction into the pleasure of expectation. Being a viewer implies this choice. The only one who cheats without interruption is the author of the film, because he has felt the approach of the threshold of irreversibility; he has even imagined that the viewer was becoming blocked, and that in order to give a little rope to the one who was hanging on, he had to fill the gaps in the film, link together the opaque fragments which will not recover their hyaline quality until they are grouped inside the viewer's pacified intelligence. The author has felt a premonition about the critical threshold; he has waited, he is waiting still. Out of prudence [but maybe it's procrastination...] the author puts off the moment when he must summon up his strength, move on to attack. He waits for the viewer to find his aptitude for diving into the unpredictable the way one dives into an inky night. The dialogue resides in that. The viewer, the interlocutor, chooses to ignore the processes that are used to cast a spell over him. Life is probably too short to let us keep in touch with the latest techniques for abduction; it's enough to be carried off. Better yet: it's enough to want to leave...)

HAMLET

I have of late – but wherefore I know not – lost all my mirth, foregone all custom of exercises; and indeed, it goes so heavily with all my disposition that this goodly frame the earth seems to me a sterile promontory; this most excellent canopy, the air, look you, this brave o'erhanging firmament, this majestical roof fretted with golden fire – why, it appeareth nothing to me but a foul and pestilent congregation of vapours...Man delights not me – nor woman neither...

Eva and Nicolas are watching the program together in the living-room of the apartment on Berri Street.

HAMLET

Gentlemen, welcome to Elsinore...Denmark's a prison.

ROSENKRANTZ

Then is the world one.

HAMLET

A goodly one; Denmark being one o' the worst.

Panoramic shot of the living-room: we recognize the pictures, the furniture arrangement. The only light comes from the television set. Eva is slumped on the sofa, staring at the screen. Nicolas unplugs it, wraps the cord around his cast and picks it up by the handle with his right hand. The camera follows this operation. In a few seconds Nicolas has set it up again on the dresser in the bedroom, so that they can watch it from the bed.

EVA

That's a good idea; now I'll be able to fall asleep watching television, since you spend the whole night writing your screenplay.

NICOLAS

Tonight's an exception: I'm watching *Hamlet* with you.

EVA

When does Fortinbras come on?

NICOLAS

At the end – in fact he's already there, but we don't see him.

Hamlet's lines come crackling out of the set while Eva, leaning against the pillows, watches the program with obvious fervour. Nicolas slips a letter-opener between his cast and his arm and rubs the skin with insensate energy.

EVA

Stop, I beg you. You're going to hurt yourself. In two days you'll be rid of your cast...

HAMLET

Ha, ha! Are you honest?

Shot of the television set: Linda Noble playing Ophelia.

OPHELIA

My lord?

The camera stays on Linda Noble. Hamlet walks around her, looking her up and down. We never at any time see Hamlet from the front.

HAMLET

Are you fair?

OPHELIA

What means your lordship?

HAMLET

That if you be honest and fair, your honesty should admit no discourse to your beauty.

OPHELIA

Could beauty, my lord, have better commerce than with honesty?

HAMLET

Ay, truly: for the power of beauty will sooner transform honesty from what it is to a bawd than the force of honesty can translate beauty into his likeness...I did love you once.

EVA

What's wrong?

NICOLAS

Don't look at me, I'm crying.

Nicolas gets up, leans against the window, not really seeing through his tears the western part of Montreal and the outline of Mount Royal.

NICOLAS

Leave me alone for a minute, I beg you.

Eva goes back to her place, deeply affected, pretending to watch the play but not even listening to the words.

HAMLET

I loved you not.

OPHELIA

I was the more deceived...

Nicolas comes back, wiping his eyes. He sits on the bed beside Eva.

HAMLET

If thou dost marry, I'll give thee this plague for thy dowry: be thou as chaste as ice, as pure as snow, thou shalt not escape calumny.

Eva approaches Nicolas and kisses his chest. She opens his shirt to kiss him again. He lets her do as she wishes, but does not take his eyes off the television screen. The picture of Linda Noble accompanies Hamlet's words like a visual counterpoint to this tissue of insults and imprecations.

HAMLET

God hath given you one face, and you make yourselves another...You nickname God's creatures and make your wantonness your ignorance. Go to, I'll no more on't; it hath made me mad. I say we will have no more marriage. Those that are married already – all but one – shall live.

OPHELIA

O, what a noble mind is here o'erthrown!...
Th' observed of all observers, quite, quite down!

EVA

Do you know that actress?

NICOLAS

Linda? Of course.

EVA

I don't like her. There's something about her...

OPHELIA

O woe is me
T' have seen what I have seen, see what I see!

NICOLAS

She did that very well: "...what I have seen, see what I see!"

EVA

She plays very coldly...Look at her eyes: the blue is so pale
her whole eye looks white.

NICOLAS

She isn't playing coldly, she's playing soullessly. And that's
even more upsetting because after this tirade she has nothing
else to say; she loses her mind. She's going to kill herself.

EVA

I know why you like her so much – well, I can guess, I mean.
She has long blonde hair; a kind of golden river flows from
her head.

NICOLAS

That's beautiful, what you just said. You know, Linda's the
person I was thinking of to play Sylvie.

Eva is startled.

EVA

There was something painful about Sylvie, something sin-
cere.

NICOLAS

Never forget this, Eva: before Sylvie threw herself into the precipice, before my eyes, on our wedding trip, she lacked sincerity.

> They are silent. Eva rests her head on Nicolas' chest; he is still watching the television screen. She unfastens all the buttons on his shirt and pulls it out of his pants.

HAMLET

'Tis now the very witching time of night,
When churchyards yawn, and hell itself breathes out
Contagion to this world. Now could I drink hot blood
And do such bitter business as the day
Would quake to look on.

EVA

I'd like to see Linda again.

NICOLAS

She won't be coming back.

EVA

Is Linda her real name or her stage name?

NICOLAS

Her name is Linda Noble.

> They are naked, bathed in the feeble light given off by the luminosity of the images, which varies in intensity and in chrominance according to the editing. Eva and Nicolas are more or less discernible on the spread, sometimes clad in a half-light, sometimes in a rubescent nudity. Their bodies are entwined, without violence, on the bed as they watch Shakespeare's tragedy.

HAMLET

Look here on this picture, and on this,
The counterfeit presentment of two brothers.

EVA

I'm watching the picture upside-down; it's even more fascinating.

Nicolas spreads Eva's legs and keeps them in that position. Eva's neck comes so close to the edge of the bed that her head and her brown hair hang down towards the floor. She sees the picture upside down and stays on the bed, clutching the bedspread with both hands.

HAMLET

I must be cruel only to be kind...

Hamlet lets out a long strident cry after this last statement. Eva's moan is a continuation of the Prince of Denmark's cry; she is groaning with love, eyes open, as she watches her own inverted version of Shakespeare's tragedy. Nicolas caresses her with his breath, as though he were giving form to a black mirror of Murano with his hand and mouth. Eva, her nipples erect, panting, continues to moan as she watches and listens to Hamlet. From Eva's open thighs we can see the variegated television picture, sometimes cut by Eva's belly as it rises, or by Nicolas' head in the foreground. Insert Eva's dangling head, then closeup of Nicolas. With his fingertips, he spreads the hair-edged lips and bites; but is he really biting? Rather he is inhaling, or avidly sucking the fleshy peak where the small lips come together, the dark pink bulb that swells and hardens in his mouth. What difference does it make how precise the shots are! The approach to this carpel in the depths of the pubic forest can only be allusive. The viewer cannot see what Nicolas only guesses and touches with his tongue, nor can he attend a show which cannot be presented, since everything takes place in the damp blackness of the groin. Under the effect of this gentle intrusion Eva begins to shout, her voice covering Nicolas', which at this moment is coming out of the television set.

FORTINBRAS

Go, captain, from me greet the Danish king.

EVA

Was that you????

140

NICOLAS

Yes, that was Fortinbras.

EVA

I saw you! It isn't over yet?

NICOLAS

Fear not, Fortinbras comes back in the fifth act, at the very end.

> Eva relaxes, the better to relish her pleasure and distress, and closes her eyes for a moment.

HAMLET

Good sir, whose powers are these?

CAPTAIN

They are of Norway, sir.

HAMLET

Who commands them, sir?

CAPTAIN

The nephew to old Norway, Fortinbras.

> Nicolas rests his cheek on Eva's belly and looks diagonally at the tragedy which Eva can see only upside down, like a *spiegebild*. For her, the characters' feet cling to the ceiling. Closeup of Eva, her head thrown back.

EVA

What are you thinking about?

NICOLAS

Fortinbras...

EVA

Is that all?

NICOLAS

You know very well that I'm still thinking about Sylvie. I was thinking that Linda Noble would play her. I try to place her on the streets of Oslo, at Tromsø, on board the *Nordnorge*, at Ny Ålesund.

EVA

Are you going back to Spitsbergen to make the film?

NICOLAS

Of course, I could shoot most of the scenes at Repulse Bay...Repulse Bay is very beautiful: the thalwegs drop off into the sea. It's a landscape with a monstrous beauty: a silent, white inferno.

> As Eva listens and watches the screen, Nicolas, whose penis is adamantly rigid, enters her suddenly just where a few moments earlier he had been murmuring inaudible words. Eva, surprised, raises her head and loses sight of the coffered ceiling of the palace of Elsinore.

HAMLET

If only there were sun this night...

EVA

Nicolas, you're going to make me miss the end of Hamlet. Wait a bit.

NICOLAS

All right, I'll wait with you, inside you.

> Eva is back on the bed. Her mouth is at the same level as Nicolas'. She kisses him, turns him over on his back and lies on top of him. Nicolas assumes the position that Eva was in a few seconds earlier.

NICOLAS

When your head's down everything becomes strange, more beautiful. I've never seen what I'm seeing now.

> Eva feels a certain relief to be looking at a picture that has been restored to the right direction. With her head on Nicolas' chest she spreads her arms to form a cross and strokes her lover's hands with her fingers. She rotates her pelvis very slowly, almost imperceptibly.

NICOLAS

Eva, I don't know if it's because I've got my head down that it's happening, but I've never felt so happy and I've never been so stiff...I feel as though I'm going to the very depths of your belly, as though I'm going to stab you.

EVA

Let me listen.

NICOLAS

Then don't move as you were doing so perfidiously, otherwise...

Eva puts her mouth on Nicolas' skin and sucks on one of his breasts.

HAMLET

I am like the shadows.

Eva lifts her head; the two do not move.

HAMLET

The world is a dream and dreams are a world.

Motionless, but as though in an unstable balance on their anchorage, Eva and Nicolas seem at moments to waver a little, responsive to some light and gentle wind.

NICOLAS

Fortinbras comes on quite soon. Eva, Eva, I'm getting enormously long inside you. It's overwhelming – as though I were grafted to you now and it can't be stopped; even my head is swollen with blood and my hair is giving off fluffy stars.

FORTINBRAS

Where is this sight?

Eva is motionless, gazing steadily at the convex surface of the television screen. Nicolas looks at the inverted picture. The editing should show the alternation from one point of view to the other, a double vision of the same show: pictures of Fortinbras inverted, Eva's eyes slightly clouded, Nicolas with his head down, then the same series in disorder. Lips revealing Eva's impeccable teeth, Nicolas' hair which seems to be an extension of the pile of the carpet, Fortinbras walking on the ceiling.

143

Men are so inevitably mad it would be another act of madness not to be mad.

Nicolas' ever louder breathing responds perfectly to the silences in the lugubrious spectacle unfolding on the screen. The Prince of Denmark's body is solemnly carried away to the muffled chords of the *Discorso*, while the entwined bodies of Eva and Nicolas, the one inside the other and the one enveloping the other, have become pillars of salt.

(At this point in the film the viewer might experience a slight feeling of security if he could see this sequence through to its logical conclusion, watch the flooding consequence of so many caresses and the frenetic solution of the crisis. But it is necessary to interrupt this process of being swallowed up, transform the two feverish bodies into pillars of salt and leave the viewer to his own unsatisfied desires and to the demands of *habeas corpus*. Instead of spreading through Eva's mucous membranes, nectar will flow through the serpiginous paths of the viewer's imagination and rise up to the invisible capitals of his being. From this moment the viewer has, in one way or another, turned around: he wonders why he has been deprived of the spectacle, a rather pleasurable one all the same, of the couple who are near the end of a rather long but still original process of caresses. So much venereal innovation to end so abruptly! It's enough to make the precarious relationship between film and viewer explode. From another point of view, this upset might carry with it an entire chain of ellipses that make it possible to go no further in the action, but to go deeper and in a constellatory manner. The sudden interruption of amorous protocol breaks a certain artificiality in the development of the film. One might say that ideally the viewer, surprised by the cut – which has coincided with the end of the televised presentation of Hamlet – is in a state of intense vigil, not because he is expecting anything particular, but because he imagines that what will follow will surprise him once again.)

Direct cut. Michel Lewandowski walking up and down Saint-Denis Street between the Chévalier cinema and the Chez Achille bar. He is easily distinguishable from the crowd by his China-white sports coat and his loosely knotted silk tie. Groups of young people from the neighbourhood walk past him, cross the street and sit at a table Chez Pablo or at the Saint-Malo. It is late afternoon and still hot. Michel Lewandowski keeps looking at his watch. A car brakes in the street, very close to him. A taxi comes to a stop, Eva gets out, radiant, very pretty in her harem pants and blue blouse. She goes directly to Michel Lewandowski: the two kiss each other on the cheek.

MICHEL LEWANDOWSKI
When are you leaving for California?

EVA
I don't know, Michel. In fact I know less and less about it. I'm staying in Montreal.

MICHEL LEWANDOWSKI
Because of him?

EVA
Yes, because of him. You guessed right, Michel.

MICHEL LEWANDOWSKI
Life is strange, really strange.

EVA
I think so too.

MICHEL LEWANDOWSKI
Sylvie kills herself on her wedding trip. You told me about it yourself the other morning near the Hotel Sonesta. You come back to Montreal and I can't help saying this, you've replaced Sylvie for him.

EVA
Have you met him?

MICHEL LEWANDOWSKI

No, I've never met him. I've seen him on television a few times, last night in Hamlet, too. Quite frankly, his acting career doesn't interest me.

EVA

He isn't an actor, not any more. He's in films now, as a writer-producer. And how about you, Michel, are you still working at the stock exchange?

MICHEL LEWANDOWSKI

No, I've started a firm of financial consultants. Quite interesting – just now, for example, I'm looking after a Dutch group that's setting up in Montreal.

EVA

Why are you looking at me like that?

M. LEWANDOWSKI

Did you see Sylvie in Oslo before the accident?

> Direct cut to Sylvie, Eva and Nicolas walking together along Karljohansgate.

EVA

Yes, I saw her.

MICHEL LEWANDOWSKI

Did...?

> Shots of Sylvie, smiling, in Oslo. The briefness of these inserts is equalled only by the progressive shortening of the closeups of Michel Lewandowski. The dual series of shots unfolds like a discordant song, some rapid shots being held too long so that the viewer, accustomed to distinguishing evocations of the past from the present track, may well wonder if he is decoding this series of shots correctly.

EVA

I only saw Sylvie and her husband in Oslo before they left for Svalbard.

Quick succession of shots of Sylvie, Eva and Nicolas in Oslo: at Pernille, on Lille Grensen, in front of the Fønix. End this series by coming back to Sylvie and Nicolas arriving at Fornebu.

M. LEWANDOWSKI

How did the accident happen?

EVA

Sylvie fell when they were climbing on Spitsbergen. That island is covered with rather high mountains.

M. LEWANDOWSKI

She fell?

EVA

That's all I know about it. A climbing accident. When Nicolas came to see me on his way back from Spitsbergen he was completely distraught.

Overexposed image: we see Sylvie falling into a precipice in slow motion. Interpolated flashes of Michel and Sylvie, sleeping together. Sylvie falls into space, tracing an infinite arabesque because of the effects of the mountain. Cut to Michel Lewandowski looking at his watch.

M. LEWANDOWSKI

I have to leave soon, but I'd very much like to see you again, Eva, and have a chat. Because you're the only person who knew about Sylvie and me.

EVA

The only one?

M. LEWANDOWSKI

Yes, the only one to share this secret with me. Perhaps we could have lunch together one of these days?

EVA

I'd love to.

M. LEWANDOWSKI

Give me your phone number.

Michel Lewandowski takes out his diary and prepares to note the number. Eva waits for a moment.

M. LEWANDOWSKI

You haven't forgotten it?

EVA

There's one other person besides me who knew about your liaison with Sylvie: that's Nicolas.

M. LEWANDOWSKI

Just what does he know?

EVA

I don't know. But Sylvie told me about it in Oslo.

M. LEWANDOWSKI

I understand. I won't call you. Because of him.

He takes a card from his wallet and hands it to Eva who puts it in her bag without even glancing at it.

M. LEWANDOWSKI

Give me a call, in the morning if you can, and we'll make a date.

They kiss. Then Michel jumps into a taxi while Eva goes back up Saint-Denis, heading north. From the other sidewalk the camera follows her in tandem. Continue this travelling shot at least as far as the Bibliothèque Nationale. Cut.

Nicolas Vanesse is working in the living room to a deafening musical accompaniment. He is wearing pale beige linen trousers and a blue polo shirt. He hears Eva come in, goes to greet her. They kiss.

EVA

What were you doing?

NICOLAS

Waiting for you.

EVA

And the screenplay?

148

NICOLAS

Didn't you notice anything?

> Eva looks all around her. She looks, moves, takes a number of different points of view, looks in the other rooms and comes back.

EVA

In French do you say I haven't got the foggiest idea? Well, I'm completely fogged in.

NICOLAS

I haven't got my cast any more!

> Eva touches Nicolas' wrist gently. Fade to black. Sylvie is in the big bedroom, the master bedroom, with Michel Lewandowski. Night.

SYLVIE

Do you want to know everything?

M. LEWANDOWSKI

Yes.

SYLVIE

Here in your bedroom, I suddenly understand that my life is over, that I'll never be happy, not even consoled.

> She bursts into tears and throws herself onto the bed. Michel Lewandowski, sitting close to her, caresses her tenderly.

SYLVIE

The house, this bedroom, your bed...

> She writhes on the bed, victim of violent convulsions. She has lost control of herself and Michel Lewandowski, shattered, looks at her, saying nothing. He tries to catch her, but in vain, because Sylvie keeps moving and does not want to be touched. Her features are drawn by her pain and moral suffering. She looks around her, examines the large bedroom where she feels lost, then seems to calm down a little. Finally she wipes her face

and, lying diagonally across the bed, her eye lights on a print just above the head of the bed. Zoom-in on the print: we can make out an old village with a waterway running beside it. We can easily read the legend: Natchez-under-the-Hill.


("I am the new Norway...")


Apartment on Berri Street. They have finished eating. Eva serves coffee. Nicolas gets up, goes to get a bottle of Williamine and a balloon glass.

EVA

Don't you want any coffee?

NICOLAS

Yes, I'll have some, but I like to compensate for the bitterness.

EVA

Compensate for the bitterness – what does that mean?

NICOLAS

Never mind, Eva. It's become a reflex for me to find a new pretext every time I drink, and a new way to say it so it's incomprehensible.

EVA

Have you decided to put Linda Noble in the film?

Nicolas downs his glass of Williamine in one gulp.

NICOLAS

It's already done. I spoke to her on the phone this afternoon. She agreed. We have to set up the shooting schedule, of course.

EVA

If you were happy with Sylvie and if she hadn't killed herself before your eyes, what kind of screenplay would you have invented?

NICOLAS

When I started writing it, Sylvie was with me, close to me –
and I couldn't find a more beautiful story than the story of a
wedding trip to Spitsbergen. A love story doesn't need a
tragic dénouement to be beautiful.

> Closeup of Nicolas repeating this last sentence word for
> word. Overexposed shot of Sylvie executing her ara-
> besque in the precipice.

NICOLAS

Tonight I have to go at it really hard and make some progress
with my screenplay.

EVA

Can I help you?

NICOLAS

Yes. Paginate the screenplay from the beginning and give me
a summary of the sequences.


(In Montreal the coefficient of the fantastic decreases percep-
tibly because everybody works. To say nothing of the fact
that the city is not splendid and excessive like Spitsbergen.
The set is no longer enormous and savage like the Arctic
islands; instead of snow-clad peaks and sliding glaciers, there
are buildings filled with people. The unbelievable passages of
the Kongsfjorden give way to the overcrowded area of Place
d'Armes near the offices of Marcus Films. Time, in Montreal,
is not an entity that can be extended or compressed. No, it is
an urban prosody. The way it is divided up increases it endlessly, but never elongates it. Everything is done according to
a collective division; Montreal is synonymous with conges-
tion, Spitsbergen with a barely circumscribed emptiness, it is
so uninhabited. The only way man has found to dominate
time has been to spatialize it *ad nauseam*. Time is the very
secret of subjectivity and if we must refer to a journey in
order to capture it more sharply, we must invoke the inner
journey. When we objectify time, we are talking about the
time of others and, consequently, of the space that separates

us from others. In love, however reduced this space may be, it still represents the impassable boundary between two beings. The inner time of the other can be perceived only at the highest point of ecstasy, as the irreducible space that separates two lovers confines them to superficial caresses and forbids them true fusion. It is difficult to render all the despair of that last sentence; if one had power one could, through the artifices of writing, surmount the inevitable spatialization of time that makes us grow older outside the duration of the loved one. We transcend time only to sink into a spatial crevasse and in the euphoria of the crossing we forget that time always moves faster than we do and that it moves in space, outside its own structure. Thus we believe that it is fleeting when it escapes through constant metastasis, but it is we who disappear. The line down the middle of a bed is even more cruel: when we have crossed it we have not crossed it! We believe that we enter the loved person: all we do is slip over the shining skin of the legs. Love, no matter how deliberately intrusive it is, is reduced to a velar approximation of the other, to a desperate cruise on the roof of a sea that can never be pierced. Here we find the corticality so peculiar to the process of the film. All existence unfolds on the fringe of time and on waves that threaten to open, but never expose more than what a consenting belly exposes to the one who invests it. It is not time that flies, it is the being who steals away; it is the others who flee and seem to be fleeing as they walk, false prophets, over the unbreakable waters of the Barents Sea. The skin of the loved one veils everything, even the person one thinks one knows because one has participated in the same delirium of obscuration and pleasure. The mirror-cantata has just shattered under the devastating action of the *cogito cogitatem*, only the shards of a two-way mirror still exist. No one knows anyone, that's certain...If there is no way to convey the sorrow contained in this last assertion, if the bumpy travelling shots do not acutely render the problems of existing on the impenetrable bark of reality, then the image is worth nothing. It is nothing and all that remains is to invent a musical substitute to express the great sorrow that we feel; a cantata for the valley of death. Sylvie, a ghost, climbs back up the precipice, reversing the choreography of her fall; the image is resorbed in its own cancellation. Spleen contaminates everything; no one escapes its bite. Let's forget the image, for the landscape is being obliterated, the white combes of Spitsbergen grow dark under the effect of a sad song. If possible, everything must be abolished, leaving on the screen only the closeup of Sylvie in despair. The rest comes from the obsessive song that replaces what cannot be represented. The image is only an absence, the negative of a cherished phantom.)

Eva appears in the doorway, holding the black notebook.

NICOLAS

It would be very nice if you'd leave your work for a few minutes and type that for me. It's the budget estimate I've just finished. I still have to do a rough diagram for the critical path I must give the company tomorrow.

Eva types. Nicolas takes notes, draws curves, writes dates and names on a large sheet of paper.

Dissolve: Nicolas getting out of the shower. He dries himself and comes out of the bathroom wearing a bathrobe.

NICOLAS

I'm not doing any more work today.

He lies down on the sofa, after putting a record on the stereo: a *Ricercari* by Gabrielli. Nicolas adjusts the volume, while Eva, who is in the bathroom, puts up her hair before getting under the shower, humming the counterpoint of what she hears from a distance. She disappears under the steaming jet of the shower. Do not euphemize the representation of her naked body. She is nude, without affectation, totally naked. Under the jet of water we see her just as she is. She shuts her eyes so the water can fall on her face.

Dissolve: The bedroom, plunged in darkness; the only light comes from the television set. Eva appears in the doorway, but we guess at her body rather than seeing it; she lays her clothes on a chair, takes out a nightgown and puts it on. Nicolas is lying on the bed, several pillows under his head; he is watching a film in French. It is not important to identify the film, except by its soundtrack: "Il était une fois dans l'ouest." Eva glances at the picture.

EVA

You know, Claudia Cardinale would be good as Sylvie.

NICOLAS

No.

EVA

You'd just have to bleach her hair, have her wear it shoulder-length...Well, all right, Linda Noble will play Sylvie. But who'll play Linda Noble?

NICOLAS

I might leave out that part. Anyway, it's not a very big one.

EVA

It isn't a big part so far, but you haven't finished the screenplay yet.

Eva sits on the bed beside Nicolas who is completely absorbed in what is happening on the screen.

EVA

I've reread everything you've written from the beginning. Do you want to know what I think of it? Some important scenes are missing.

NICOLAS

For instance?

EVA

You skip over Sylvie's suicide. She kills herself, that's stated quite clearly, but we aren't there when it happens except through the intermediary of Nicolas' account.

154

NICOLAS

You're right, I think – in fact I was wondering about the same thing. Did anything else strike you?

EVA

Yes, the dialogue – it's cumbersome and a little artificial, it seems to me.

NICOLAS

I'm delighted to hear you say "artificial." I want dialogue that will be more articulated, more complicated than the exchange of lines we've become used to. For me, dialogues that ring a little false have the power of rendering the fantastic more effectively than realistic conversations can do. The kind of reality I'm representing in the film includes conversations like the one we're having at this very moment. Pseudo-naturalism in dialogues generally impoverishes their tenor and reduces every verbal exchange to an exchange of stereotypes. When dialogue is brought back to the natural it has no other function than that of lubricant. I have a completely different idea about speech in life: speech gives birth, it does more than simply ornament or accompany existence.

EVA

Another point: it seems to me that it's not just Sylvie's suicide scene that's missing from the screenplay in its present form; there's also a lack of explanation about Hamlet, Fortinbras and their meaning in the context of the film.

> Nicolas smiles briefly, gets up, mechanically adjusts the contrast and brightness of the television, comes back and lies down beside Eva.

NICOLAS

Did you really miss that?

EVA

Yes; I even wondered if all those remarks about Hamlet had any meaning. I wondered if you hadn't inserted that element simply to mystify the viewer and if in the end you weren't going to let him down precisely when he's expecting the final word.

NICOLAS

That's funny, what you're saying. You're really reacting like a viewer on the attack. And you want to be sure your attack is a valid one! I find your remarks really interesting. That question about Hamlet and Fortinbras, for example.

EVA

What is the truth?

NICOLAS

Right now, the truth is that I'm falling asleep. I'm even prepared to pass up Claudia Cardinale.

> Nicolas turns off the television and lies down, eyes shut. Eva gets up and turns the television on again: the picture quickly reappears. The film's musical theme bursts into the room, in full force: a long, sustained note which divides and spreads through the desert. Eva stays on the floor, leaning against the bed, close to the television set.

NICOLAS

What's going on?

EVA

Nothing. I'm watching the film: the colours of the desert are really superb. The sand isn't blond, it has a reddish tint.

> Nicolas sits up, bends his head so he can see the picture. Closeup of Nicolas looking to the right, towards the back of the room. He gets out of bed and goes to the wall which is covered from floor to ceiling with books. As Nicolas jumps out of bed he takes a wrong step which causes him to trip against the bookshelves. He bends double in pain; he takes a few steps and crumples onto the bed, holding his left wrist. Eva leaps up, goes to him.

NICOLAS

It hurts. I've broken my wrist again. I'm sure I have. How stupid.

EVA

Why did you jump out of bed so...?

(Nicolas' comments end here. He is dreaming again, of Amlethus, Ammelhede, Amlaidhe, Amlodi, Amlairh, Hamnet, Hamlett, Anleifr, Hamblet, Amlaigh, Anlaf – and of Fortinbras who took this assumed name from the king, Fortinbras, who had no children and knew of the existence of Hamlet's twin. He adopted the cursed son Amlethe, appointed him his dynastic heir, protected him and persuaded him that on the death of Claudius or of his twin he had only to unmask himself and he would become king of Denmark. King Fortinbras, through the intermediary of his protégé, would thus extend his empire over Norway and his worst enemy, Denmark. Fortinbras' reign was of brief duration and through a historical ambiguity, he was buried under the name of Fortinbras in his own country, at Undensacre, the very place where little Amlethe went when he met his own death far from the Danish coast. Fortinbras' grave is to be found at Undensacre or in the Undensacre. But no one knows with certainty where Undensacre is. The historian Sigurd Sigurdson puts it in the same place as Odense, by rearranging the phonetic structure of the ancient name to make it similar to the name of the capital of Fyn. Odense and Undensacre are not evolutive antinomic terms (not in appearance at least), but the possibility of their convergence is non-existent when one knows that they were part of the same language at the same period. At first glance, Odense has one advantage: verisimilitude. For in order to go from Sjealland to Fyn one has only to cross Samso Baalt or the Nyborg Sund. But this geographical contiguity does not authorize any proximity if we insist on etymology. Undornsakrar, a likely derivative of Undensacre, means south cape in Norwegian. And at those latitudes, the southern cape can only be at the north. One need only reread Arnoldus Tylensis, Dudo and all of the Gesta Danorum to understand that Undornsakrar can only be the extreme south of the extreme north. Now Odense is not south of Fyn, but right in the middle; moreover, the city does not overlook the sea and bears no resemblance to a cape. Undensacre, where Fortinbras' grave is found, has nothing to do with Odense. There is no question of dogmatically locating the grave of

Fortinbras, nor of inventing a place which might have been the goal of the first (fictitious) voyage of Amlethe and the end of his last one. No! For the moment, it is important to emphasize that there has been a symbolic shock in the screenplay. Fortinbras, heir to the throne of Norway, finds himself king of Denmark before becoming king of Norway, while Nicolas Vanesse, Fortinbras once removed, takes possession of Eva Norway before he inherits her. Perhaps the variant is more concerned with temporality than symbolic valences. Let us continue. Anyone who has read the last lines of this commentary will understand that what he has spent a few seconds reading cannot, in any way, be incorporated into the script. The references to Arnold of Thule and to Sigurd Sigurdson cannot be translated into images. It is possible to transport melancholy onto the giant screen, to see the infinity of the desert in the viewfinder, to frame what is invisible to the naked eye, but it is absolutely impossible to translate into an image speculations about the secret relationship Queen Gertrude might have had at Undensacre, in the very place where her son was buried. Besides, the reader has also just realized that the screenplay he has read from the beginning is embedded in the present commentary and that this commentary explains the publication of that which it enshrines and reproduces, structurally, the stratagem of the play within the play – but inside out. It is not an insertion of the smaller within the larger, but of the larger within the smaller, which generally evokes an idea of contraction. Now, contraction is a good definition of the process of writing, while cinematographic production implies a dilation. When choosing between these two movements whose repeated addition is nothing less than the principle of peristalsis, one has a tendency to select compression only so far as it can then be dilated, setting aside from the beginning anything that cannot be acted upon. Dilation does not necessarily result from the contiguity of what is volatile; some condensations may well lead to full flowering. The compression of the imagination, for example, has the same effect on the pupil of the eye as atropine: it dilates. Everything, finally, dilates and opens to the extent that one has soon forgotten the contraction that preceded the expansive joy. If this commentary is coming to an end, and when it does come to an end, it does not mean that the screenplay is no longer framed by it. From now on the reader knows that the screenplay overlaps a commentary that cannot be interrupted. But that which stops might continue so that which continues had stopped; beginning again postulates stopping earlier, a provisional break. The screenplay suggests a counter-response; it is inseparable from the subject that frames it and from the counter-subject grafted onto it, just as it feeds on the response from which it emanates. All in all, the screenplay is caught within a frame, invisible at first, which shows itself to be more encompassing and more extensive. However, one must not lose sight of the fact that the screenplay, subordinated to this complexus, is not yet developed, that when the film is completed it will be completely woven into the film's commentative texture. This is another way of saying that the narrative will not be completely enshrined until the framework is invisible. The play within the play has metamorphosed into a film inserted into an uninterrupted study of Undensacre. Contrary to all appearances, the directionality of this gloss is continuous and, for the moment at any rate, incomplete. The search for the grave of Amlethe-Fortinbras goes on, from Sylvie's open thighs to Eva's garlanded breasts, and on to the black eyes of Claudia Cardinale who flies, an impure bird, from tree to tree in this discursive forest, which resembles despair.)

The television is still showing scenes from "Il était une fois dans l'ouest": a river of sorrow, abandoned to itself is flowing. And the landscapes suspended from the breasts of Claudia Cardinale recall the Poliads, divinities of ancient Numidia: Ghar es-Zemma, the virgin desert, El Kenissia,the fertile desert, Bou Kourneim, the celestial desert. What is the importance of the sands of Tipasa and the dunes of Sainte-Salsa, when all these expanses, under the effect of filters, resemble the fine

sand of Undensacre and the black snow of Spitsbergen?
Eva, sitting on the floor, trembles as she watches the end
of the western; on the screen she sees Sylvie who, like a
negative, walks blondely through a cold desert, barely
avoiding the precipices – one of which, we know now,
will be her grave.

EVA

What's the name of the town where Sylvie's sister lives?

NICOLAS

Black Lake.

EVA

Will you take me there some day?

NICOLAS

All right, but don't ask me to go and visit Charlotte and her
husband.

EVA

I'd like to meet her. As a matter of fact, who's going to play
her?

NICOLAS

I haven't thought about it yet. It's a small part.

EVA

You haven't thought of asking her?

NICOLAS

No, I hadn't thought of that.

EVA

It would be very suitable because she looks like Sylvie.

NICOLAS

Perhaps you've forgotten that she doesn't look like Linda
Noble.

EVA

That's true. Sylvie won't be Sylvie.

The harmonica sets up strange syncopations which
make sleep impossible.

EVA

There's another important part in your screenplay, even though he doesn't appear; that's...

NICOLAS

What character do you mean?

EVA

Michel Lewandowski.

NICOLAS

I thought...Oh well! I thought of getting in touch with the gentleman and suggesting it to him outright. But that's madness. Besides, quite frankly, I'm looking for the actor to offer the part to.

EVA

Is the television bothering you, Nicolas? I mean, is it keeping you awake? Because I'd like to watch the Sergio Leone film to the end. I must say, it's very nice to watch television at night. In Norway the programs finish at 11 p.m.

She turns back to the set.

Direct cut. Small screening room in the Marcus Films building, on Place Royale. Screen tests are being projected. We see Linda on the screen. She is walking, smiling, putting on makeup in front of the camera, sinking into a chair. The camera comes closer to her, takes a very tight shot. We hear on camera:

NICOLAS

Lights.

Then the colour spectrum passes over Linda's face. She says nothing. Still on camera:

NICOLAS

OK Linda, that's all for you.

The film is still running. There is no kind of editing; we even see the universal leader on the film before going to a medium shot of Eva. She starts her screen test by taking off her raincoat. She walks, dances, smiles, puts on makeup. She is shot in closeup. She looks at the camera.

EVA

You know, I love you much more than you think...hvis man ikke koenger er Lerre over sig self, gjor man bedst i at skyte sig...

The lights go on in the screening room.

TONY

What does that mean?

NICOLAS

Something like: "I prefer suicide to life without love." She's not an actress, you can see that; she has a certain awkwardness.

TONY

As far as I'm concerned that doesn't bother me at all, Nic, far from it. The girl's really marvellous – it's a pleasure to see her on the screen.

NICOLAS

So long, Tony. And thanks for coming.

Fade to black.

Sylvie, in a Spitsbergen setting, looks up and opens her lips partially, offering her mouth to the lens of the camera. Then she is still.

SYLVIE

This time, don't frighten me.

Shoot the same sequence in the opposite direction, in slow motion: Sylvie's open mouth closes at the same time as her face moves away from the lens and her eyelids close.

Cut to the apartment on Berri Street. Gabrielli's *Ricercari* can be heard throughout the apartment. Nicolas is lying on the living room rug. Inexplicably, he rolls over to the wall, stopping at the sofa. Camera subjective from Nicolas' point of view; an oblique shot of the living room; Eva appears leaning over backwards, in low angle. She is coming in from outside.

EVA

What are you doing on the floor? Don't answer. I know you've had too much to drink and you feel safe when you're crawling. It's surer.

Eva turns, to go and change her clothes most likely. A hand clutches the hem of her dress. She turns towards Nicolas, obviously irritated. She tries to free herself. Eva breaks away, but we can hear a tearing sound. Nicolas has ripped the fabric of her dress. She finally escapes Nicolas' clutching hands.

EVA

What's happening to you, Nicolas?

NICOLAS

Nothing.

EVA

The worst thing is that you seem quite sane.

Nicolas finally gets up (he hasn't drunk too much) and sits on the sofa. Eva takes off her skirt, puts on a mini-skirt.

EVA

I wonder what's got into you, treating me like that?

NICOLAS

You think I'm being aggressive just because I want to take you in my arms.

EVA

This is the first time I've seen you smile today.

NICOLAS

I'm thinking about the film. First of all, you've got your part.

The cameraman thought you were superb on screen – and to be perfectly honest, so did I.

Eva runs over to Nicolas, sits on his lap.

EVA

You aren't fooling me?

NICOLAS

I swear.

NICOLAS

It's all set. The production company is working – and even if they're bugging me a little about the budget, the shooting schedule, etc, I've really got just one problem: to finish the screenplay!

EVA

Bravo, Nicolas!

She kisses him.

EVA

To tell you the truth, I get stage-fright when I think I'm going to be in front of a camera.

NICOLAS

Basically, I have to go into production before I've finished all the dialogue and the breakdown of certain scenes. That bothers me a little, but apparently I'm not the first person to operate that way.

Detailed retake of the scene in which Nicolas is tearing Sylvie's dress. The scene breaks down. Sylvie looks terrified. She moves away from the lens at an impossible speed. The image becomes scrambled.

NICOLAS

As far as Sylvie's suicide scene is concerned, you were absolutely right. I have to compose it and insert it into the action. And I'm blocking there – I'm not getting anywhere. That scene nauseates me as soon as I start working on it. It's very difficult. Just now, before you came in, I'd started to do some work on it, but I finally dropped it. My hands were shaking – you can't imagine...

EVA

Is that why you were lying on the rug?

NICOLAS

I don't know. Yes, yes, that's why. I was afraid of falling into the precipice, too.

Nicolas gets up, goes to pour himself another drink. He comes back, looking serious.

NICOLAS

Writing that scene is really terribly upsetting. I tore up all my rough drafts.

EVA

All you have to do is write the scene exactly the way it happened.

NICOLAS

I know. I'll get there – eventually.

Eva, smiling, sits beside him on the sofa. Looking into his eyes, she slips her hand inside the bathing suit Nicolas is wearing. He lets Eva caress him. His features are impassive. He is still holding his glass of scotch at eye-level.

Closeup of Nicolas, the glass in the foreground. He groans slightly, without opening his mouth. We hear him breathing evenly and very deeply, but the cadence of the film slows down – so much, in fact, that Nicolas seems petrified. The motion of his eyelids and the dilation of his pupils are just perceptible in closeup. His eyes close and at the same time he drops the glass he was holding. We do not hear the glass strike the floor, or anything else. Cut on this closeup.

Shots taken in Michel Lewandowski's car as he is driving into the parking lot at Bill Wong's restaurant in Montreal. He parks the car, quickly gets out and goes over to open the other door. Eva gets out of the car. They walk towards the front door of the restaurant.

Restaurant. Interior. The maître d' leads them to a table on a mezzanine overlooking most of the restaurant and the tables lined up along the large bay window.

M. Lewandowski

Two Negronis.

With a flicker of admiration Eva observes the setting in which Michel Lewandowski seems so perfectly at ease: the wall is splashed with a riot of purple and black ideograms. Michel Lewandowski is dressed in a blue serge suit with broad stripes. He is wearing a ruby-coloured shirt and a large-patterned tie, a mixture of red and blue. His sartorial elegance is in close harmony with his solid face and his greying hair.

M. Lewandowski

Since we saw each other at the Saint-Malo the other day I've been going through a file that contains a film synopsis, a budget and a list of actors' names – including yours.

Eva

How can that be? I don't understand.

M. Lewandowski

It's simple. Marcus Films asked our company for financial advice. One of my associates, the one who looks after Marcus, asked me to have a look at the file and give him my opinion.

The waiter arrives, courteous, and puts the two Negronis and the menu on the table.

M. Lewandowski

I didn't have any trouble identifying the brown-haired Norwegian woman who suddenly appears in the story and replaces Sylvie, especially because you haven't changed the first names. I even know what your fee will be.

167

EVA

Are you more or less involved in the production of the film?

M. LEWANDOWSKI

Less rather than more. My company is just involved with outside financing and management.

> Direct cut. Michel Lewandowski's large bedroom (scene already evoked): Sylvie is rolling on the bed and looking at the engraving over the head of the bed. Close shot of the engraving. The legend is clearly visible: Natchez-under-the-Hill. The lines in the etching are cloudy.

> Michel Lewandowski is eating spareribs with garlic sauce. The sauce inevitably gets on his fingers, which he licks with a hint of gluttony before dipping them in a bowl of lukewarm water placed on the table for this purpose.

EVA

Right in the text of the screenplay your name is written out in full.

M. LEWANDOWSKI

I know. But all he knows about me is my name. He's never seen me. You aren't eating much, Eva!

EVA

I'm not very hungry.

M. LEWANDOWSKI

A little vin rosé, then.

EVA

Thanks, I've had enough.

M. LEWANDOWSKI

I haven't; I find this really very tasty.

> Michel Lewandowski downs glass after glass of wine and attacks every course with equal gusto.

> Direct cut to Sylvie, her head thrown back on the snow; she is wearing nothing on her head. Her blonde hair

falls in waves on the powdery snow. She is shaking her head as she looks at the sky as though, after a strange pain, she is reaching an intolerable threshold of pleasure. During this single shot of Sylvie, the sound track is that of the Chinese restaurant: we can even hear the sound of Michel Lewandowski chewing and the sort of sucking sound with which he removes the flesh from the little bones.

MICHEL LEWANDOWSKI

Do you really believe that story about Sylvie's accident on Spitsbergen?

EVA

You're very strange, Michel.

MICHEL LEWANDOWSKI

I probably phrased my question badly. I just mean that it seems very improbable in the script. Mind you, I've only read a summary. But it's too big an accident under the circumstances. Don't you think so, Eva?

EVA

Because it happened.

M. LEWANDOWSKI

Suicide would be better than that accident. More morbid, but more interesting, perhaps.

Closeup of Eva.

EVA

In the summary they only talk about the climbing accident?

M. LEWANDOWSKI

What? Was there actually something else?

EVA

No. No, Michel. A summary just has to be shorter.

M. LEWANDOWSKI

Still, murder would be the best solution. The wedding trip interrupted by a murder. The couple destroyed at the very

169

moment it is being formed in intimacy...

> Eva looks at Michel Lewandowski with horror. Her
> hands are trembling; she is obviously deeply affected
> and sits stiffly in her chair, staring.

(Michel Lewandowski is right; the viewer has not waited for
this meal at Bill Wong's for nothing. Murder is better than
suicide because it reveals a pure intention to destroy. To kill
during a wedding trip is the most devastating reversal of love:
inauguration is transformed into an absolute end. It is not
strange for Michel Lewandowski to arrive so quickly, through
his imagination, at this tragic end! He has lost Sylvie, who was
his lover, and he has lost her a thousand times because she
went on a wedding trip with a twenty-eight-year-old man.
Michel Lewandowski is forty-nine. Because he loved Sylvie
and because she has left to celebrate her union with Nicolas
by going to Svalbard with him, Michel has, no doubt, deep
down inside himself, wished for Sylvie's death, and he has no
trouble imagining that Nicolas Vanesse brought her not love,
but death, despicably premeditated. Through his own pain
Michel Lewandowski has been quick to deduce the most appropriate conclusion to this catastrophe which has relegated
him to the confines of his age – doubly so because Sylvie and
Nicolas belong to the same generation. But one of them no
longer exists. These few lines are added to the commentary in
which the strands of the plot are woven together. The viewer
can only guess at the network that follows the screenplay like
a shadow, or precedes it when the sun moves behind the characters' backs and makes the screenplay run after the film
rather than going ahead of it. When the commentary goes
back inside the crystalline corpus of the story the Iceland spar
is no less luminous, but the shadow that once appeared will
return, restoring the periodic procession of the screenplay to
the system which encloses and dominates it, to the point that
the screenplay cannot be understood if it is dissociated from
its inextricable armature. Some constants appear: Svalbard,
Undensacre, Natchez-under-the-Hill, Repulse Bay, Montreal,

170

Oslo. Michel Lewandowski wanders through these different sets; he is looking for a new one, one that belongs to him. He is not in search of an author, but a set: a new city, or several glaciers plunging slowly into the vortex of the Barents Sea or even a periglacial platform where he might analyse the digitation of the Magdalenefjorden, all the while reflecting on the futility of a fiction which is intelligible only if it is approached through what it is not.)


Bill Wong's restaurant. Interior. Almost empty. It is nearly three o'clock in the afternoon.

M. LEWANDOWSKI

Tell me more about her.

EVA

That's all. I didn't see her for long in Oslo. And Sylvie, as you must know, was secretive; she didn't confide in people easily.

M. LEWANDOWSKI

Losing her is even worse if I have no more memories to feed on. Love needs memory if it is to grow deeper and endure. At the moment I'm dying of hunger. Sylvie is dead and she's dragged me into the precipice with her.

Direct cut to the apartment on Berri Street.

NICOLAS

He didn't suggest a quick trip to a motel?

EVA

That's unfair, Nicolas. When we finished lunch he brought me back to the city. He was crying as he drove.

NICOLAS

Is that all?

EVA

No. Nicolas, don't forget that it's out of loyalty that I've brought you the comments of one of the characters in your film. Because I know how concerned you are to arrange things so that the screenplay is composed only of what really happened.

Nicolas continues to write on the large sheets of paper all that he has drawn from his conversation with Eva. Then he staples the sheets together and puts them in his desk.

EVA

You know he has two grown-up daughters?

NICOLAS

Vaguely.

EVA

The younger one is about twenty, and her name's Sylvie – Sylvie Lewandowski, that's pretty.

NICOLAS

No, I didn't know that.

EVA

What did you finally decide about the murder?

NICOLAS

I'm going to wait a few days. For the moment it's no, because I don't want the screenplay to turn into fiction in the end. Something else: I am royally annoyed at Monsieur Lewandowski sticking his nose into this film.

Eva is preparing to go out: fan-pleated skirt that comes half-way down her thighs, faille weskit, sunglasses. From the bedroom, she asks Nicolas:

EVA

Will it take long to find all the locations?

NICOLAS

We have to count on at least two days in Montreal, maybe three. Afterwards...

Underground garage of the apartment building on Berri Street. Nicolas throws his key-chain to Eva.

NICOLAS

Will you do me a favour and drive? My left wrist's still too weak.

They get into the Ford Torino; the car climbs up the ramp and comes out onto Berri Street.

Dissolve: the car is heading west along Maisonneuve. Cut to the Central Station, gate 11. Michel Lewandowski is standing at the gate as the New York Central train arrives. The passengers get out. Long shots: we see Michel Lewandowski, from the front, cut through the crowd and go towards a young woman who throws her arms around his neck. She has blonde hair. Another long shot in the inside parking lot at the Central Station. We recognize Sylvie beside Michel Lewandowski. We recognize Michel Lewandowski's car too. They get inside.

Nicolas takes several pictures of buildings on Drummond Street, near Pine Avenue. Then he gets back into the car where Eva is waiting.

EVA

What do we do now?

NICOLAS

Turn left on Sainte-Catherine. Take the Bonaventure Expressway. We're going to Nuns' Island.

EVA

Are you making any progress?

NICOLAS

Not much. Now I'm looking for a place that I haven't written into the script yet.

Series of shots of the car stuck in traffic on Sainte-Catherine Street, on University Street beside Place Ville Marie. Dissolve: the Ford Torino has stopped on the grounds of the Port of Montreal's administration building, alongside the St. Lawrence, in the same place where the scene between Nicolas and Sylvie took place when she asked him to drive all night to Natchez-under-the-Hill. In the fresh air Eva and Nicolas begin to relax.

NICOLAS

I'm very preoccupied with everything I still have to do on the screenplay. And the idea of Sylvie's murder is tormenting me. I tell myself that Michel Lewandowski might be right, strictly speaking. (And thank you again for telling me what he said.) But that would upset my screenplay too much, since I've been building it on the truth. I still see Sylvie running full speed towards the precipice and myself, like a cripple, unable to do anything but shout, trying to hold her back. One thing's sure, I could never imagine myself pushing her.

Eva comes over to Nicolas, kisses him on the mouth, takes his right hand and places it on her thigh. She slips her tongue between his lips. Nicolas moves his hand up under Eva's blouse and cups her breasts. Closeup of Eva. Her face is marked with sorrow.

NICOLAS

What's wrong?

EVA

...sometimes I feel as though I'm in the way.

Swish pan to the interior of Michel Lewandowski's house. Sylvie, beaming, is taking off her stockings by rolling them down to her heels; then she removes the stocking from the other leg with her foot and they fall onto the rug in the big bedroom. She lies on the bed, still wearing her skirt and brassiere.

Direct cut to the Ford Torino. The car is driving onto Nuns' Island. Dissolve: Eva drives the car alongside a terrace overlooking the St. Lawrence. Nicolas gets out of the car, takes pictures of the whole street, of houses, then, signalling to Eva to wait for him, he goes into a high-rise. Nicolas takes the elevator and presses the button for the top floor, at random. The doors open at the

174

top floor onto a huge, brightly lit laundry room. Nicolas goes into the laundry, crosses it. At the other end, glass doors open onto a terrace; Nicolas is rather surprised to discover this superb lookout. There is a wooden railing around the terrace and Nicolas leans over, sees the Ford Torino far below. He has a bird's eye view of a charming section of Nuns' Island where there are only two-storey houses. He adjusts his lenses, sets the aperture and places the viewfinder to his eye. Image from the viewfinder: a sort of haze in which we can, however, distinguish the form of a gabled house with wide windows. He focuses on a large window in Michel Lewandowski's house; we can make out a silhouette which is closing the double curtains. Cut.

The large bedroom. Closeup of Sylvie who has just given Michel Lewandowski a long kiss.

SYLVIE

Two months is a long time.

Shot of Sylvie and Michel: he is undressing her with great delicacy. Naked, the lovers entwine and move between the sheets, in the middle of the bed and under the engraving of Natchez-under-the-Hill. Very tight closeups of Sylvie and Michel. Their expressions are serious, intense.

SYLVIE

This can't go on any longer, papa. It can't go on!

She kisses him repeatedly, on the cheek, the neck, the lips, with desperate haste.

SYLVIE

Papa, papa, papa...

MICHEL

You're right, Sylvie, it can't go on.

(Until this moment, the viewer has decoded everything. Suddenly what he was keeping at a certain distance by means of his shadow-measurer enters him violently; suddenly he understands that Michel Lewandowski, who has been Sylvie's lover, was also her father, so that at the end of this enigma there is only one Sylvie, and the only link which, from the beginning of the film, allowed this tragic equation to be established was the engraving of Natchez-under-the-Hill and not the surname of the woman who is buried in a ravine on Spitsbergen. Sylvie, lover and daughter of Michel Lewandowski...The sudden revelation cannot allow the viewer to get back on his feet in a few seconds, or even to understand how this is really possible, given the various elements in the screenplay which he already knows. But it is nonetheless true that the viewer's brain has just been bombarded by solar particles charged with electricity and that the walls of his skull are suddenly being swept by blank images.)


SYLVIE

This can't go on, papa. Someone could find out. Nicolas, maybe. You never know.

MICHEL

It's impossible for him to know, absolutely impossible. But you're right, Sylvie, it can't go on. You'll resent me for the rest of your life.

SYLVIE

I resent you now, for waiting until I was twenty-one.

They assume a position of double fellatio, Sylvie lying with her open legs on her father's shoulders. For a few seconds the camera is on the engraving of Natchez-under-the-Hill. We hear the couple moaning in a flashing synchronism. A long silence. Breathing, nothing else.

SYLVIE

Papa, it's terrible.

Cut.

Eva is waiting by the Ford Torino, taking a few steps. Nicolas suddenly appears on the sidewalk in front of her.

NICOLAS

The view from the roof is really extraordinary. I think I've found what I've been looking for. A house, isolated by trees, fairly large...

EVA

What do we do now?

NICOLAS

Let's leave the car there. I want to have a closer look at that house, cover all the angles and take some reverse shots to see what kind of picture it gives.

The bedroom in Michel Lewandowski's house. A diffused, very soft light illuminates the room. Closeup of Sylvie Lewandowski's face. One might think her pierced by arrows like St. Sebastian.

SYLVIE

Papa – this is the last time; it has to be.

Closeup of Michel Lewandowski who is stroking his cheek against Sylvie Lewandowski's downy pubic hair. He comes even closer to the sanctuary, opens with his lips and fingers Sylvie's Venusian involucre as though seeking the seed of all life in the depths of that blonde umbel.

SYLVIE

Come inside me, come...

MICHEL

Yes. But this time, hold me tight inside your armilla and let's not move.

SYLVIE

Let's never move again.

Michel Lewandowski is on top of Sylvie; they are looking deeply into each other's eyes. She begins to cry softly.

MICHEL

When you sob it makes you hold me even tighter. But don't cry, Sylvie, hold me.

SYLVIE

Papa, do you think I'll ever be happy?

MICHEL

I want you to be – forget what's happened between us.

SYLVIE

Forget it...

MICHEL

I want you to forget it. And I want you to be happy with Nicolas; perhaps one of these days you'll even marry him.

SYLVIE

I am happy.

MICHEL

Come on, Sylvie, you mustn't let yourself be overcome by sorrow.

Sylvie Lewandowski looks at her father, smiling.

SYLVIE

Look – I've stopped crying.

MICHEL

What are you doing to me, Sylvie? What are you doing to make me so happy?

SYLVIE

Hawaiian women have an extraordinary technique, apparently, for keeping their partners erect inside them all night long. I read about it...

They kiss each other gently on the mouth.

SYLVIE

Papa, I feel like crying again.

MICHEL

Cry, you'll feel better afterwards.

SYLVIE

Do you know what I need, Papa? A drug against life. Because I'm monstrous.

MICHEL

We've only consoled ourselves about life, nothing more. Don't turn into a tragic little girl again. Don't sob that way, Sylvie. And I'm just on the verge but I don't want to come inside you right away, I want to stay inside you as long as possible, forever...

Sylvie Lewandowski calms down a little and stops crying.

SYLVIE

This is the last time.

MICHEL

Yes.

SYLVIE

Is there snow in Hawaii? The snow is so soft. My childhood is filled with snow. It never stopped. And I thought it was so marvellous when you walked through the snow. The big snowflakes blinded me. And when it was too much for me you'd take me in your arms. Do you remember that, Papa?

Sylvie throws her head back. Upside-down shot of the engraving of Natchez-under-the-Hill. The engraving looks as though it has been subjected to a milky emulsion in which it slowly becomes its own negative.

SYLVIE

I can feel you inside me right up to my heart; you're touching everything that I am. You're everywhere, Papa, everywhere. Help, Papa! Kiss me. Life is disgusting.

Cut to exterior. Nicolas, one knee on the ground, is taking location shots around what he does not know to be the house of Michel Lewandowski, when he was looking for a house which could be Michel Lewandowski's.

Montage of shots, almost allusive, of Sylvie Lewandowski and her father, in the bed; insert shots of Nicolas circling Michel Lewandowski's house in a network of fixed frames.

(Nicolas has, then, located an imaginary house which he wishes to use as though it were the real house of Michel Lewandowski and, through a certain irony of fate, the house is the actual dwelling of Michel Lewandowski. However, a false simultaneity is suggested to the viewer between the scene taking place in the master bedroom and the process of locating the house, because Michel has not looked outside, any more than Nicolas has really noticed his shadow near the window. When all's said and done, the preparation of the film unfurls at the level of fiction (for what is not known is fictitious, isn't it?), whereas the screenplay itself is based on truth. And what happened at Nuns' Island is a new combination of the truth-fiction motif: fiction broader than truth because it is undetermined, accidentally encompasses the truth.)

Interior. Michel Lewandowski's house. The shots of the couple are off centre, increasingly illegible, the lighting is inadequate, the image out of focus. We can make out only Sylvie Lewandowski's cheeks streaming with tears, her hair spread over the pillow.

High-angle shot from the apartment building at the south of the island, not far from the Champlain Bridge, from which we can clearly see Michel Lewandowski's house and Nicolas, walking around it, towards Eva. They move away from the house.

(The screenplay is written in the present inexistential. The present is used on paper, but when each sequence in the film has been shot, it will be conjugated in the past. This discordance of tenses only emphasizes the subordination of the screenplay – or of the narrative – to the commentary surrounding it. The present in the screenplay is like a porous infinity.)


Apartment on Berri Street. Nicolas puts his location shots on the sofa.

NICOLAS

Eva, come here.

Eva comes in from the kitchen, wearing a mini-skirt. She walks through the strange museum where blow-ups of the locations have been arranged.

EVA

Fantastic. That house on Nuns' Island is really very beautiful.

NICOLAS

If you've had a good look I'll put everything away now.

EVA

OK!

Nicolas puts all the pictures into one pile.

NICOLAS

Because I have to write the final scenes for the screenplay tonight.

EVA

But do you know what time it is?

NICOLAS

I know, I know – but I have no choice.

EVA

Can you stay awake all night?

NICOLAS

Probably. In fact, I've decided on the solution for the murder. I've finally decided to kill Sylvie. Don't you think it's strange that after starting out in the autobiographical mode I'm finishing this screenplay by masking the truth?

Eva strips naked as she goes to the bedroom. Nicolas tidies his papers; he opens the black notebook and sits on the living room sofa. Cut.

The *Nordnorge* is approaching Longyearbyen, a mining camp on the nival band that separates Isfjorden from the massifs. This is the administrative centre of Svalbard. The site of the installations testifies to it. The *Nordnorge* comes to rest in the glacial Ponza which is Isfjorden, a spot of morbidezza. The gangplank is immediately lowered. Nicolas rushes out. He walks down the long street that has no delimitation but the position of the buildings, and spots the economart. He goes in, buys alcohol, other supplies and a large sharp knife. He returns to the wharf with his bag of supplies. Sylvie is waiting for him on the deck.

NICOLAS

What woke you up?

SYLVIE

I don't know – probably the engines stopping.

At this moment the engines begin to rumble again. Dissolve: the boat slowly leaves the concrete wharf. Sylvie and Nicolas are standing on the deck. The *Nordnorge* is heading northeast and is under weigh, like Micipsa in a trance, towards Pyramiden, the archaean double of Djebel Amour. The Isfjorden reflects what defines it, like a floating psyche. The set of the Spitsbergen ceases to be a set, so much does its disproportion escape any decorative function. Superimposed: shot of Nicolas scribbling in his black notebook. Return to Isfjorden: the *Nordnorge* is still cutting across the fjord with the sharp edge of its hull, advancing through this white universe which is never truly white: the drifting pieces of ice are streaked with blue, the water contains the colours of the mountains, the mountains, covered with ice and snow, have walls of schungite flecked with yellow and red.

(The viewer knows now that Nicolas Vanesse has chosen to bring about Sylvie's death by murder. Factual suspense is dissolved by this single revelation: the viewer's attention moves at once to other fields. It is important now for him to understand this sudden chrysalidation of the plot. Suspense has a bearing on the course of the murder, not the way it might be carried out. Besides, Nicolas has envisaged killing her by pushing her into the precipice. But whatever method is used, he still must find a homicidal concatenation to take the place of a last-minute justification. *Odi et amo*...Is it possible to push Catullian virulence to the point of murder? Perhaps, after all, when we recall how he was betrayed by the madwoman he was mad about...)

Closeup of the engraving of Natchez-under-the-Hill. The village contains about twenty wooden houses crammed between the cliff and the turbulent water of the Mississippi; two paddle-boats are tied up in the harbour. There is only one street and it runs parallel to the river. At the end of the street the walker may gently enter the waters of the Mississippi and baptize himself by immersion until his body, purified of the spirit of evil, turns liquid and rolls like the waves of the great river as far as Bâton Rouge, Plaquemine, Chalmette, Evergreen...The camera pulls back a little and reveals Sylvie Lewandowski lying on the bed, naked. She is asleep. Her father turns on the shower in the bathroom. Sylvie Lewandowski rises up on her elbows, realizes that she is alone in the big bedroom, and naked. She gets up, dresses, rushes towards the bathroom. She hesitates before going in, leaning against the door-frame. She knocks on the door. The sound of the shower can still be heard as well. Sylvie Lewandowski knocks again and opens the bathroom door part way.

SYLVIE

Papa...

The shower is turned off.

SYLVIE

What are you doing in the shower? I thought we...

MICHEL

You were asleep, Sylvie. Anyway, you know very well...

SYLVIE

Finish your shower. I'm taking the car to the drugstore. I won't be gone more than ten minutes.

MICHEL

The keys are in my desk. Be careful.

Sylvie moves away. The camera frames her very tightly: her head fills the entire image. She walks steadily. She leaves the room, crosses a landing brightly lit by daylight. Sylvie Lewandowski picks up the two suitcases she had brought back from the Central Station. Cut to exterior. Sylvie leaves the house, moving quickly; she walks past the car, not even glancing at it. She runs without stopping as far as the bus-stop at the corner of Claude Bernard Street. She arrives out of breath, panting.


(It might be better for the reader who is waiting until the end of the story to make love with an impatient partner to put a bookmark between the pages here. Books close and open without pain, with no problem, a slight cracking of the spine at the very most. Besides, they see nothing: they are objects, as blind as their authors. Come on, a nice break! It will be easier to concentrate afterwards, and tackle what is about to happen in the story.)


Reception desk, Hotel Bonaventure. Sylvie Lewandowski is filling in a registration form. The clerk examines it politely and adds her name in block letters.

CLERK

Madame Lewandowski, is that correct?


SYLVIE

Yes; Madame Sylvie Lewandowski.

Dissolve. She is in her room, beside her still unopened suitcases. She goes into the bathroom. She kneels beside the bathtub which is filled to the brim; she searches in vain for her reflection in the transparent water. Underwater shot: Sylvie looking towards the bottom of the bathtub. Then the water is stirred up; Sylvie's blonde hair is soaked in the water and her head, thrown back, is completely submerged: a mask of horror and distress pulls her skin towards her forehead, making the drowning woman's face even smoother.


(An aesthetic of insertion and superimpression underlies the film. The twisting of motifs cannot completely mask this formal mutation which makes the film, as well as the suspense, change objective and lose its representational function. The film will not end as foreseen. The illuminated theatre is no longer illuminated; even worse, it is not a theatre. The Ionic columns, the latticed windows, the gilded appliques, the skylights, the crimson curtains do not constitute the reality they purport. The edifice is cracked, as though reduced to being only its own ruin. What was gradually fitted into the plot takes on the appearance of a tragic collage: murder is superimposed on suicide, just as the false accident at the beginning was subsituted for suicide, and the love between Sylvie and Michel Lewandowski has been inserted like a foreign body into a story which suddenly becomes increasingly foreign to its initial plan. The body of the screenplay is swollen by these diverse means; it has lost its primary identity and now is crystallized on the submerged face of Sylvie Lewandowski.)


185

A new day is flooding the Berri Street apartment: Nicolas is lying on the loose sheets of paper where he makes notes as he writes. The black notebook is also open on the living room rug, beside a bottle of Chivas Regal. Nicolas is sleeping soundly. Eva, wearing a nightgown, comes over to him. Her glance falls on the note near Nicolas' face. Very tight closeup of Eva: her expression is one of dread. She picks up the pieces of paper that are practically touching Nicolas' face, withdraws without taking her eyes off Nicolas and closes herself inside the bathroom. Medium shot of Eva seen through the mirror: she is softly closing the door. Eva does not even look at herself in the mirror. She reads, stupefied, the pages she is holding in her hands; her mask dissolves. She starts to read the first sheet again. Closeup of Eva. Illegible flashes of the manuscript.

EVA

Sylvie will die the way she did die; change nothing, modify nothing. The acts must be carried out slowly and to the very end, including...

Closeup of Eva: she looks up from the text and sees herself in the mirror. Eva places her trembling mouth against the mirror, her lips meet her lips, her eyes, her eyes.

EVA

Poor Sylvie, poor Sylvie.

Eva takes her lips from the mirror as though tearing herself away from a kiss. She picks up the papers again, rushes out of the bathroom. She goes directly to Nicolas who is still asleep. She puts the papers back beside Nicolas' head, then opens the curtains, the window. Nicolas moans.

EVA

When do you want me to wake you?

NICOLAS

Eleven o'clock.

> As he says this he turns over to find a more comfortable
> position. Dissolve to the Ford Torino. Eva is driving. The
> car is heading downtown. Nicolas is silent; with his
> head leaning against the window, he watches the out-
> side world go by.

EVA

And what about Sylvie – did you kill her in your screenplay?

NICOLAS

I spent the whole night trying to find a way to kill her. I didn't
come up with anything good and now I think I'm just going
to leave the murder blank in the screenplay. I'll have lots of
time to devise that sequence between now and the start of
shooting.

EVA

I'd understood that...your character would push Sylvie, push
her into the precipice.

NICOLAS

You misunderstood. I said that I didn't see myself pushing
Sylvie into the precipice.

EVA

Nicolas, could I see Linda Noble, in the flesh?

NICOLAS

Sure. Let's invite her to dinner one of these days, next week
maybe.

EVA

Fine. But since you'll be seeing her this morning, in your
office, I thought...

NICOLAS

It's a tiny office – and Linda will just be dropping in to sign
her contract.

EVA

I see. You want to keep me away.

NICOLAS

I thought you were going downtown to shop, that you had a lot to do. Now I know! Come to the office and I'll introduce you to Linda Noble.

> Nicolas gets out of the car in front of the entrance to the company's offices on Place Royale. Eva drives the Ford Torino to the municipal parking lot on rue des Commissaires. She leaves the car and runs back to Place Royale.

> Dissolve. Eva goes into Nicolas' office. A music track drowns the beginning of this sequence. Nicolas is facing Eva, who is shot against the light, and Linda Noble is sitting in a chair in a shadowy corner, set back. Suddenly Eva sees her: smiling, her blonde hair falling over her back and shoulders, impressive. Nicolas introduces them. Linda Noble's beauty dazzles Eva, there is no doubt about it. The wings of her nose, so finely sculpted, the dark eyes, the oval of her face, her slender figure, her presence – all these details which Eva takes stock of with her eyes, while Linda Noble, Nicolas and she find themselves in this room with a depressed ceiling, looking out on the Port of Montreal.


NICOLAS

I have to go to the accounting department for a couple of minutes. But wait here for me.

> Nicolas leaves his office.


(The present is being used here to take an inventory of what is lacking. This tabulation evokes lacunae, gaps, omissions, absences.)

> Eva is putting clothes away in the bedroom of the apartment on Berri Street. Nicolas arrives unexpectedly. He grabs Eva between her legs and tries to throw her onto the bed. After a loveless struggle he attains his goal, smiling, a joker.

188

EVA

No, not now.

Nicolas kisses her on the mouth. Eva tries to get away.

NICOLAS

What's wrong?

Nicolas, overexcited, is trying to find the hooks on Eva's dress. She gets up and runs to the bathroom.

EVA

I'll be right back.

Medium shot of Eva from the bathroom mirror. She takes off all her clothes, looks at herself with blasé curiosity. She approaches the mirror, opens her mouth and gives herself a kiss.

EVA

Poor Sylvie...

She leaves the bathroom, naked, resigned, almost offering herself. Parallel travelling shot to the bed where Nicolas is waiting for her. Eva rolls towards the middle of the bed and when she is on her back and Nicolas straddles her, covering her, Eva slips rapidly under him so that her head is under his solar plexus and her hands are on his penis.

EVA

Get on your knees.

Eva's hands are on Nicolas' groin; she exerts an uneven, vibrant pressure on his penis. We realize that Nicolas is quickly reaching a level of excitement that is almost unbearable.

NICOLAS

Let me come inside you.

EVA

No. Not until you tell me the truth. How is Sylvie going to die in your film?

NICOLAS
I'll tell you afterwards, let me come inside you.

EVA
Talk! That will help you control yourself.

NICOLAS
In the precipice...

EVA
You're lying.

NICOLAS
I stab her and then I throw her into the precipice.

EVA
Come inside me now, come.

> Nicolas does so. The image turns cloudy. We hear him shout almost immediately, from the height of his orgasm.

(Sequences with a high sexual content may seem to be an excess as useless as they are irritating for the viewer unaccustomed to reading films. This is unfortunate. There is not enough emphasis on the formal expressiveness of sex in the cinema and on its correlative in art history, the nude. The cinema confers an impressive plastic agitation on everything that it denudes, and specifically because of this it invades the imagination of a viewer who would be left cold by the Venus Anadyomene. There is a certain ambiguity in this. For if the colour film projected onto a large screen exposes naked bodies, in one movement it can immediately remove them from sight. The cinema, like time, steadily annihilates what it represents; the naked bodies have scarcely been shown when already they are abolished, freeing the screen for other images. Thus one should not judge the scene which has just taken place between Eva and Nicolas as though it were a fixed object, able to be observed from several different angles and slowly contemplated. The nude, rediscovered during the

Renaissance, is in a way extended in the cinema, but by conforming to the annihilating laws of time. Moreover, this is only a question of an extension of the principle of the greatest expressiveness. When we express, we seek to express as much as possible, not to clothe in a starry cloth a reality which has no firmament. In the last scene between Eva and Nicolas, nothing occurs except what might lead, pitilessly, to an outburst of truth. The few nude scenes scattered through the film convey a melancholy which is otherwise difficult to render, for naked bodies in an embrace possess great eloquence. The kisses one gives, vague caresses, clutching so savage and disorganized, only make the flight of time more agonizing, for the hand running over a thigh will soon reach the end of its course and lips joined in a kiss will soon end their mutual palpation. As is the case in music, there is never an identical reprise; when bodies are reunited the memory of previous embraces is erased by the new emotion. Everything begins again because everything comes to an end; and the melody which never resembles itself completely brings us closer to a final embrace, which abolishes everything.)

Interior. Shelter. Spitsbergen. Sylvie, partly undressed, is helping Nicolas unfold a tent canvas, near the fireplace where a fire is burning. The meal is finished.

SYLVIE
How will we know when it's tomorrow?

NICOLAS
What difference does it make?

Sylvie lies down on the improvised couch. Nicolas slips Sylvie's ivy-red sweater under her head as a pillow.

NICOLAS
Close your eyes!

SYLVIE
Why are you asking me to close my eyes? I don't like that!

NICOLAS

Close your eyes, Sylvie.

> Nicolas is smiling at her. Sylvie closes her eyes. Closeup of Sylvie's hand, which Nicolas is tying with a piece of rope. Establishing shot. Sylvie is struggling furiously.

SYLVIE

What are you doing with that rope? Let me go!

> But Nicolas has already tied Sylvie to an iron hook inside the fireplace (which is used for hanging kettles) and in a flash he cuts the rope at this second knot. He moves quickly to do the same thing with the other wrist, which he fastens to a supporting joist.

SYLVIE

Nicolas, why are you doing that? Nicolas?

> Sylvie's voice becomes pleading. Nicolas is kicked in the temple as he prepares to tie Sylvie's foot. It makes him fall to the ground. The struggle begins again, worse than ever, but Sylvie has only her legs against Nicolas who, to protect himself, starts with Sylvie's head and finally ties her ankles to two other joists by the same process. Sylvie is firmly bound, her arms and legs spread. There is a horrified silence.

SYLVIE

Why did you do that? Why?

> She is weeping. Nicolas, sitting close to her, puts two logs in the fire and stirs it up carefully, impassive as though Sylvie's pain does not even touch him.

SYLVIE

Nicolas, this is our wedding trip. We've come all the way to Spitsbergen and now look what you're doing! Stop, I beg you – you're frightening me and I'm in horrible pain.

NICOLAS

It hurts me too.

SYLVIE

Here, untie me and come into my arms. We'll comfort each other, love, even if I don't understand you any more.

Nicolas looks absent, distracted, but it isn't real absentmindedness; and not absence either.

SYLVIE

Tell me what's wrong, Nicolas. And even if you don't open your mouth I forgive you in advance for tying me up like this, because you must be very unhappy to be doing what you're doing.

Nicolas looks at her for a long time, silently. He touches her forehead, her cheeks, lets his hand wander over Sylvie's body.

NICOLAS

Something irretrievable has been spoiled.

SYLVIE

But what have I done?

NICOLAS

Michel Lewandowski... At the very moment we had decided to come to Svalbard together, to join ourselves together for life, you saw him again!

SYLVIE

But Nicolas, I admitted to you that I'd been wrong – and you forgave me.

Nicolas rests the back of his neck against Sylvie's stomach and looks into space.

SYLVIE

Stop touching me.

NICOLAS

He touched you, he touched you everywhere. When you swore that you'd always love me you'd just come from his arms!

SYLVIE

Nicolas, you're a monster!

> Nicolas gets up slowly. He has already stopped hearing Sylvie's cries, which are more and more piercing. He kneels between Sylvie's thighs. He bends down and puts his mouth on Sylvie's blonde pubic hair. Closeup: with his left hand he spreads the outer lips. We can make out the gleam of a blade which enters her vagina and touches her clitoris. He proceeds to perform an introcision. Closeup of Sylvie, her mouth open, face contorted in pain.

NICOLAS

From now on your life is spoiled too.

> Blood is pouring from Sylvie's vulva.

SYLVIE

Love, perhaps there's still time to mend everything, start over again.

> As she speaks, with desperate gentleness, Nicolas is delicately sticking the point of his pocket-knife into her pubic hair and bringing it up towards her navel which he encircles with a red line, then up between her breasts. The cut is not deep.

SYLVIE

Love, I beg you. Stop while there's still time.

> Nicolas bends down and puts his lips on the tip of her breast. He stays there for a long time, sucking her breast. He moves to suck the other breast.

NICOLAS

You've told me that I didn't know how to kiss your breasts. But your father knew how.

> He is sitting close to Sylvie's head.

SYLVIE

You're raving, Nicolas.

NICOLAS

I'm not raving. Michel Lewandowski is your father.

SYLVIE

Where did you get that idea? We don't even have the same name.

NICOLAS

Because nobody knows that your name is really Sylvie Lewandowski.

SYLVIE

Michel Lewandowski isn't my father.

NICOLAS

After your parents were divorced you changed your name. You took your mother's name, Dubuque. That way you were able to introduce Michel Lewandowski to your friends; no one could penetrate your secret. When you took the precaution of changing your name officially you were sure that everything had been erased.

SYLVIE

How do you know?

NICOLAS

One night when you thought I was asleep I heard you pleading with him on the telephone. You kept saying, "No papa, not tomorrow, it's risky."

Nicolas makes a cut at the corner of her mouth and continues the line to her earlobe. He does the same on the other side of her face. Sylvie is weeping bitterly. She seems to be wearing a mask, the cuts are so much more pronounced than her own features.

NICOLAS

Don't move.

Rapidly this time, Nicolas makes two slanting lines on her forehead. Muscles of chagrin. With his fingers, he pulls on these thin strips, but there is too much blood gushing out of the cuts. With his knife he draws pouches under her eyes.

NICOLAS

Poor Sylvie, your tears are red.

> Nicolas is obviously sad; he is crying too. He bends over Sylvie to kiss her breasts again.

SYLVIE

I'm cold Nicolas, I'm so cold.

> Nicolas raises his head to look at her. He sees her face all streaked with blood, her false smile, the muscles of chagrin which have become bloodless and the two bloody pouches under her eyes. He places the tip of the knife under her left breast, then sticks it in. She is dead. Nicolas withdraws his knife, puts it on the bloody canvas. Nicolas gets up, dresses to go outside. He picks up Sylvie's clothes and covers her with them, like a shroud.

> Dissolve. He unfastens the cords which had bound Sylvie and folds the canvas over her.

> With broad, quick motions he ties her up like a sausage. Nicolas acts precisely.

> Dissolve. Nicolas drags the green canvas bundle over an icy surface. He is barely straining. A short distance from the shelter there is a precipice. Nicolas places Sylvie's body parallel to the edge of the precipice. Twice he pushes her to make her roll to the edge. The third time, Sylvie Lewandowski's body slides slowly and falls into the void. Nicolas walks away but he has an attack of vertigo. High angle shot of him walking back towards the precipice, with terror, as though he can't stop and as though the precipice were exerting an irresistible attraction over him. He staggers, falls backwards; his head is very close to the precipice. Fade to black.

> Place: Linda Noble's apartment (this is not known to the viewer). Linda is feverishly reading a photocopy of the screenplay.

LINDA

There are some pages missing, that's obvious. They've been torn out.

EVA

I know. Michel Lewandowski read them to me today, before he gave me this photocopy of the screenplay which he got directly from Marcus Films. He destroyed the pages after he'd read them. When I have the strength, Linda, I'll tell you what's in those pages.

Eva is wearing a dark brown bolero; Linda is wearing a broad poncho of printed cotton, and under it she has on only her slacks, no blouse or brassiere.

LINDA

Eva, it's only a script. You imagined that Nicolas really killed his wife, but I'm sure it didn't happen that way.

EVA

Nicolas told me over and over that everything in his script was absolutely true.

LINDA

Except for the murder!

EVA

The murder too. I read a note he'd written: "Sylvie will die the way she did die. Change nothing."

LINDA

Anyway, your theory about the murder can't be checked. Besides, this murder seems like a crime by a raving lunatic; it's grotesque.

Linda hands a drink to Eva who is sitting in a white leather chair which contrasts with her tanned skin. Linda sits on the other side of the living room, on a sofa.

EVA

Another thing. It was when I read the screenplay that I found out that Sylvie Dubuque was Michel Lewandowski's daughter. I met Michel Lewandowski the first time I visited Montreal. He was Sylvie's lover, nothing else, as far as I was concerned. Frankly, I envied Sylvie for being squired around by someone so seductive, so handsome and refined.

Linda Noble's apartment is very soft to look at: the colours range from eggshell to chestnut. Eva willingly allows herself to be seduced by the sensuous ambience in which everything seems to conjure up violence and murder.

LINDA

I admit quite frankly that everything about a certain Linda Noble in Nicolas' screenplay is true, except for a very few details – and that only corroborates your theory. I'm not very proud of myself when I think about all that. And you, you had every reason to despise me too. Why did you insist on coming to my place tonight?

EVA

To warn you of a danger.

LINDA

I don't understand.

EVA

Nicolas wants to start the shooting with the final scene.

LINDA

As a matter of fact he told me the same thing.

EVA

I wanted to stop you from being his next victim!

LINDA

Come on – the cutting with the knife, that could certainly be faked in the film.

EVA

We might as well admit it: killing Sylvie with the knife would be possible, but eating certain parts of her body the way he did...

Flashes. We see Sylvie Lewandowski tied down, quartered. She has been cut in several places and is bleeding copiously. Her forehead is monstrously open. Closeup of Linda Noble. She is overwhelmed.

LINDA

I can't believe it.


(Linda Noble is shaken because it is she who plays Sylvie Lewandowski in the film and also because the producer of the film, Sylvie's murderer according to Eva Vos, has also bound her, Linda, to a bed. And now she will be bound again, in order to play the part of Sylvie Lewandowski. What Linda did not understand about Eva's behaviour in the beginning now seems increasingly clear to her. Now that Eva Vos has disclosed the murder scene, the film seems unproduceable except at the cost of a murder: Linda's. Nicolas' venture looks like that of a madman. For Linda it is no longer a question of untangling reality from fiction, because the fiction is inextricably linked with reality, and by dissociating one from the other Linda will no longer know, in the end, if it is the fiction that she is isolating or what may inappropriately be designated as reality. This time it is the reality which is contaminated by an even more horrifying fiction. Sylvie Dubuque has replaced Sylvie Lewandowski, but now Sylvie is discovering her nominal identity in her father's arms and in the viewer's eyes. Nicolas Vanesse, jealous of the lover she has kept, seen and seen again, discovers that the man is Michel Lewandowski, father of Sylvie. The couple sets off on their wedding trip to Norway and the Svalbard archipelago masked from each other: Sylvie is not Sylvie and Nicolas knows her unspeakable secret. Eva Vos, blind mediator between Sylvie Lewandowski and her father, between Sylvie Dubuque and her husband, between Nicolas Vanesse and Michel Lewandowski, understands everything, precisely because of this final state of affairs which has caused her to follow Sylvie in the bed of Nicolas Vanesse, and which has placed her between the great love of Sylvie and her husband. Yes, Eva understands. It might be presumptuous to say that Eva understands everything, but she was panic-stricken when she learned about the complete screenplay which, paradoxically, was given to her by Michel Lewandowski (whom she did not know, until this day, to be the father of Sylvie), and particularly when the passage about Sylvie's manducation was read to her. Michel Lewandowski invited her to Bill Wong's a second time today. He could not prevent himself from crying when he read the passage in the screenplay where Nicolas sucks the blood that flowed after the introcision and the blood from the muscles of chagrin, an alkaline, slightly salty liquid which did not quench him. After lunch at Bill Wong's restaurant, Eva and Michel Lewandowski separated quickly; Michel Lewandowski told Eva that he would try to meet Nicolas Vanesse that afternoon and that, in any case, he would never denounce him to the law because he himself felt too guilty, and just as monstrous, as though he too had sucked his daughter Sylvie's muscles of chagrin before killing her.)


Linda Noble's apartment.

LINDA

When he ate Sylvie she was still alive, is that right?

EVA

Yes. It's natural that at her age certain parts of her body would be quite tasty. That's what Michel Lewandowski told me today.

LINDA

Eva, may I call you *tu*?

EVA

Oh, yes!

Eva bursts out sobbing and hides her face in her hands. Linda comes over to her, touches Eva's neck affectionately.

LINDA

Get a grip on yourself, Eva. You're safe here with me. You
can spend the night. Because now I'm the one who fears for
your life if you go back to Berri Street.

EVA

Thank you.

Eva takes Linda's hand in hers. Linda slips to the floor,
at Eva's feet.

EVA

I want to call Michel – Sylvie's father – because we left without even saying goodbye. And if I may, I'm going to tell him
I'm at your place.


(Michel Lewandowski has not received Eva Vos' call. An
hour earlier he rushed out of his twelfth-floor office on rue
Saint-François-Xavier. It is one of those old buildings without central air-conditioning, where you can still open the
windows. Michel Lewandowski has left no message, no letter, nothing. Since then, there has been a gap of several days:
Nicolas realized that Eva would not be coming back when
Linda asked him, through her agent, to terminate her contract
with Marcus Films. Other actresses were hired to replace
Linda Noble and Eva Vos.)


Direct cut to Linda Noble's apartment. Eva is in the
kitchen washing the dishes. The front door opens. Linda
Noble appears, all smiles.

LINDA

Here, I've got your suitcase. I went to the Marcus Films office
for it.

EVA

You're really very kind to me.

Eva takes the suitcase and puts it near the cupboard.

Linda, visibly tired, takes off her shoes and lies on the living room sofa.

LINDA

Do you think it's true that Sylvie tried to kill herself at the Hotel Bonaventure?

EVA

Why do you ask me that?

LINDA

To know just how much of Nicolas' screenplay is true.

EVA

Yes, it's true. Michel Lewandowski told me.

LINDA

I've got some news. Nicolas Vanesse chartered a plane from Nordair and he's leaving for Repulse Bay tomorrow.

EVA

So he's going to make the film. And because he's alive, he'll look innocent.

LINDA

In any case, I'm terrified of him. Ah! I can still see him, tying me up in Stan's apartment.

EVA

Stan Parisé?

LINDA

He's a strange guy. We haven't seen each other since I left him. Sometimes he calls me in the middle of the night, because he's afraid of the dark and he finds the nights are more and more destructive. He was a friend of Nicolas.

EVA

Forget him! And let's forget Nicolas too – and let him go and make his film at Repulse Bay!

LINDA

Now that you've got your suitcase I imagine you'll be leaving.

EVA

Why do you say that?

LINDA

Because you took refuge here to escape from Nicolas – and now that he's gone...

> Eva kneels on the rug. Her head bowed over Linda, she runs her hand gently over her face.

EVA

Crazy! I'm staying here with you!

> Eva presses her lips to Linda's closed eyes, then places her cheek against her breasts.

EVA

I can hear your heart beating.

> Linda holds Eva's head against her breast. Series of closeups of the two women.

EVA

You can't imagine what's happening inside me. It's marvellous. For the first time in my life I'm suffused with peace.

> Linda slips onto the rug. They are leaning against the sofa, looking at each other as though they are simultaneously entering a new life of which they had suspected nothing. Linda kisses her partner with infinite tenderness.

LINDA

I can't find the words to tell you what's happening – and I'd like to be able to tell you in your own language.

EVA

You too, then? For how long?

LINDA

I don't know. Here, just now, when you touched me...

> Dissolve. The two women are naked, lying on Linda's bed, radiant, at peace. Eva, leaning on one elbow, looks into Linda's eyes.

EVA

Have you ever loved another woman before?

LINDA

Never. You?

EVA

I haven't either. You're so marvellous, you know, and so
gentle. I never would have guessed...

LINDA

You and I must have been really flayed.

EVA

Why do you say that?

LINDA

I feel as though we're bandaging wounds.

EVA

But there's more than that. We've entered an infinite mutual
creation through love and we're penetrating each other with
female seed.

LINDA

When I was thirteen I thought that girls had wet dreams.

EVA

And I thought that when I made love I'd produce great
quantities of foamy sperm. Today I have the feeling that
you're transmitting a fermentive liquor to me. I feel myself
a woman made fecund – totally replete.

LINDA

So am I, and radiating in you at the same time.

EVA

When you come to my country I'll take you to Undensacre.

LINDA

Where's that?

EVA

No one knows exactly, but you and I will find it.

Eva puts her tongue on Linda's partly opened lips; she

closes her eyes in bliss. Eva puts her tongue in Linda's mouth and the two women are welded together by their embrace.


(They have already set off together on the road to Undensacre, but it is far away. And most important, no one knows whether this Undensacre is another designation for Odense or whether Undensacre is not located, rather, in western Jutland where Gertrude went, secretly, to find Fortinbras, Hamlet's twin, rather like the way Sylvie Lewandowski, when her name was no longer Sylvie Lewandowski, would go sometimes – but never often enough – to Undensacre for secret meetings with her father. No one really knows the site of Fortinbras' grave, which Eva and Linda seek in their amorous drifting; nor will anyone ever find Sylvie's grave: Sylvie, a particle of what has fled and what will follow, lies now in the eternal snows of Spitsbergen. The Island of Spitsbergen is a reverse image of Undensacre or Undornsakrar, or, again, of Odainsaker which is very far from the castle of Elsinor. While the entwined bodies of Eva and Linda walk along the illluminative way, it appears increasingly obvious that the Undensacre of Fortinbras coincides with the Odainsaker which is a suspensive vision of time.)


Eva and Linda are engaged in a caress which proceeds slowly, as though the present were dulled by their blissful slowing down. They do not leave each other, yet they continue to take each other.

EVA

There's a pale down, almost invisible, all over your body.

LINDA

And down there your hair is so thick, so dark, you seem impenetrable. You are virgin and you will always be virgin. Ah! I feel old because I met you so late in my life.

Linda allows herself to be kissed all over her body, blissful. When Eva lies on her again Linda turns her over.
Her blonde hair falls into Eva's dark hair and she, in
turn, lets herself be loved in a present which extends to
her own nothingness, constantly renewed.


LINDA

Christ is reincarnated in you.

EVA

We have crossed over the boundary of the prodigious and we
have lain togther naked in a field of asphodels.

LINDA

Jesus, burn me, annihilate me.

EVA

My soul is lost in your mouth.

LINDA

The more I drink of your being the thirstier I become.

EVA

Now true love has come. I have never felt so close to God. It's
as though I've been intoxicated by a divine poison.

LINDA

And I have swallowed the same love potion.

EVA

Now that I have seen you and I am in you and you in me, I
know what love is. God may be all in all, Saint Paul said...

Linda caresses Eva's thighs with great gentleness and
places her mouth on her vulva. Eva's eyes are open and
she soliloquizes in a low voice.

EVA

God is within me and I am entering God. I feel I am inhab-
iting him. When your tongue darts into me you lift the veil
that separated me from the milky way, and now I am almost

touching the great silence where life is born and dies and is born again on the cosmic scale, filling the void with a murmur of joy.

(There is no doubt that Eva, whose French is limited, has crossed the threshold of improbability, carrying along with her the reader who gives himself up, in spirit, to what is burning in a ramous canopy, forever and infinitely swollen as though all the branches were lifted synergistically beneath the pressure of a single, unique kiss which is not the kiss of death but rather the kiss of life and of love. The Word has entered her. The person who, like Eva, contemplates this cavernous splendour is consecrated to death. He too must die each time, be born again and try to approach even closer the pleroma which is moved back from second to second by the breath of the spirit. The way is the way of love; it moves through the lips like breath and escapes with a throbbing force which, without enlarging the opening of the lips, makes them communicate with all that vibrates, with all that shudders, with all that lives in the kingdom of Christ. Eva's pleasure is incomplete, for Eva is already moving around the celestial equator, not because the pleasure she receives from her sister is not thrilling, not because Linda's kiss is not enchanting or her tongue incendiary, but because beyond the passion which is shaking her, Eva is embracing God himself (at the same time that she is being embraced by Linda) and is being consumed in the love of love. Love causes vertigo, but her vertigo, unbearable as it may be, is an infinite delight. Anyone who has got this far knows that he is not looking at a film with his viewer's eyes but a book – one which he continues to leaf through, trembling. And this same reader has already gone too far within himself not to allow himself to be invaded, like Eva, by the final kiss which becomes infinite as soon as mutually fertilizing pleasure gives access to palingenesis and its course overlaps the eternal Communion. Let us flee to our only homeland! May the plenifying life which has woven these fibrillae, these anciform ribbons, these white wings of the soul, continue eternally towards the omega point, which we attain only at our death when we lose all identity, to be reborn and live in the Christ of Revelation. Time devours me, but from its mouth I draw my stories, from its mysterious sedimentation I draw my eternal seed. Eva and Linda are approaching the illuminated theatre where the play which is being performed is a parabola where all human works are enshrined.)